Carol V.D.

This book was a group effort. Thanks to Rich for writing and giving the small group talks. Special thanks to Maggie Baxter putting her heart and soul into writing the devotionals. Thanks to Rudy Alexeeff for being our general editor and producer. Thanks to Kyle Benedetti, Xavier Smith, and Shawn Tegtmeier for the filming process and editing of the small group videos. Thanks to Dana Hazen for contributing to editing and writing the group discussions. Thanks to Scott Engebretson for thoughtfully crafting the group prayer ministry times. Most of all, thank you to all who enjoy this series. It was prayerfully crafted with you in mind.

With gratitude,
Amanda J Nash & Paige Goslin, Campaign Co-Directors
and Rudy Alexeeff, Curriculum Director

The Real Jesus Small Group Video Series and Workbook
Vineyard Columbus

Published 2017 by
Vineyard Columbus
6000 Cooper Rd
Westerville, Ohio 43081

vineyardcolumbus.org
smallgroups@vineyardcolumbus.org

© Vineyard Columbus
All rights reserved. No part of this publication may be reproduced, stored in a retrieval system or transmitted, in any form or by any means, electronic, mechanical, photocopying, recording or otherwise, without the prior written permission of the copyright owner.

Scriptures taken from the Holy Bible, New International Version®, NIV®. Copyright © 1973, 1978, 1984, 2011 by Biblica, Inc.™ Used by permission of Zondervan. All rights reserved worldwide. www.zondervan.com The "NIV" and "New International Version" are trademarks registered in the United States Patent and Trademark Office by Biblica, Inc.™

TABLE OF CONTENTS

4	_____	Welcome Letter from Rich Nathan
5	_____	How to Use This Workbook
7	_____	How to H.O.S.T. a Group
8	_____	Group Agenda Each Week
10	_____	Tips for a Great Small Group
13	_____	The Jesus of History
20	_____	Devotional for The Jesus of History
33	_____	Jesus the Teacher
40	_____	Devotional for Jesus the Teacher
53	_____	Jesus the Healer
60	_____	Devotional for Jesus the Healer
73	_____	Jesus the Revolutionary
80	_____	Devotional for Jesus the Revolutionary
93	_____	Jesus the Suffering Servant
100	_____	Devotional for Jesus the Suffering Servant
113	_____	Jesus the King
120	_____	Devotional for Jesus the King

I am so grateful that you have decided to participate in our 2018 discipleship campaign, The Real Jesus. We named it The Real Jesus because so many people struggle with a false picture of Jesus derived from bad religious raining and inaccurate traditions. Jesus is, in the simplest sense, a real person. Jesus is someone who existed in history and powerfully impacted the lives of thousands of people in his day and continues to impact millions today. Whether you have been following Jesus for years or you are just curious about who Jesus is, my desire is that this series will help you will discover the Real Jesus and who he wishes to be for you.

During these six weeks, I encourage you to read through the Gospel of Mark. This workbook includes devotionals that will highlight a passage from the Gospel reading for that day. There is also a small group discussion guide. You'll get the most out of this material if you commit to a small group for these six weeks. My preaching on the weekends will complement this material. We'll be focusing on these same topics together as a church family across all of our campuses, from kids to adults. We also have student material as well as a family devotional available.

Before you begin, I would like you to take few minutes to pray and ask God what He might be wanting to show you about himself. What role of Jesus might God highlight for you right now? Jesus was the wisest teacher, the most compassionate healer, the most just revolutionary and so much more. My hope and prayer is that God would fill you with his Holy Spirit and help you see Jesus as he really is. May God bless you, and may God draw you closer to the Real Jesus!

With All Affection,
Rich Nathan
Senior Pastor
Vineyard Columbus

THE REAL JESUS

HOW TO USE THIS WORKBOOK

The Real Jesus was designed as a whole church series. There are weekend messages that correspond to the videos used in conjunction with this workbook. We encourage you to step fully into an experience that will challenge you, stretch you, and grow you. Our groups are designed with a holistic discipleship model. We want our groups to spend time in scripture, fellowship, worship, prayer ministry, and service. Authentic relationships that involve all of these pursuits will result in balanced spiritual growth. Each week in your small group you'll watch the video, discuss the questions provided, pray for one another, and are encouraged to read five devotionals each week.

Small Group Discussion Guide
Each week will follow a basic pattern with brief starter questions, an outline of each video message that includes the Bible passages, and a few fill-ins. After the video, there will be a few discussion questions that correspond to the message.

Prayer Ministry Time
We encourage all groups, regardless of your level of experience or practice, to pray for one another each week. There will be prayer prompts each week that can act as a guide during this time. Don't worry if you don't get through each prompt! In fact, the HOST should feel free to pre-select preferred prompts before the group meets. If you are unsure how to lead this time, watch our training videos found at: vcsmallgroups.org or call your HOST Support Team member.

Daily Devotionals
There are five daily devotionals that correspond to the weekly topics. These devotionals will inspire and challenge you as you reflect on The Real Jesus. Each day starts with a reading from the Gospel of Mark. For those who want more, each day has a "Digging Deeper" section.

Committing to the various elements of this series (small group attendance, watching the teachings, discussing the questions with people in your group, praying for one another, participating in the service project, and reading the Bible passage and devotionals each day) will not only clear up some of the clutter surrounding the person of Jesus, but will help you embrace the important roles Jesus desires to fill in your life. If you miss doing one of the devotionals or don't get through all the discussion questions in group, don't worry! The Real Jesus is gracious and compassionate! He desires devotion and not perfection.

THE REAL JESUS

HOW TO H.O.S.T. A GROUP

The easiest way to start a new group is to invite two to three friends to do this with you—that's enough! You could also invite family, neighbors, or co-workers. HOSTing is simple. It is explained with the acronym made popular by Saddleback Church in California:

H.O.S.T.
Have a heart for people.
Open your home (or provide another space).
Serve a snack. (You may want to invite others to help after the first week.)
Turn on the video.

There are helpful videos that go into greater detail about the ins and outs of HOSTing found at:
www.vcsmallgroups.org/h-o-s-t-training-videos/

Once committed to the basics of being a HOST, there are a few other tips that will help your group:

- Regularly attend. Especially when a group is still forming and in its early stages, showing up each week can greatly enhance your experience and the experience of others.

- Establish and abide by a "start time" and "end time" for group. This respects both people's schedules and the margins in your own life.

- Read the Bible passage and daily devotionals for yourself.

- Pray throughout the week for yourself, your group, and the church.

THE REAL JESUS

GROUP AGENDA EACH WEEK

Groups will inevitably have varying structures based on their preferences and the time they've spent together as a group. Below is a description of the sections included in this workbook to serve as a general guide for your time together as a group:

Social Time (10 minutes): This is a great time to get to know people and serve coffee with snacks.

Getting Started (10 minutes): Have each person say their name and respond to the opening question or questions.

Worship (10-15 minutes): Vineyard historically highly values worship. Many of our current Vineyard small groups take time to worship. (This is optional for The Real Jesus: A Person, Not a Religion series.) Worship is the response of the people of God, to the person of God, because of the glory and goodness of God. It is true that worship can take many forms and that worship involves the very way we live our lives. It is also true that worship is a spiritual practice of the will. Worship involves the mind, body, and soul. For these reasons, Christians throughout history have practiced worship in poem and song. We see this clearly stated in both the Old and New Testament. If the leader or someone in the group is able to play an instrument, we encourage that this talent be used in group!

Alternatives to live music include singing along with a music track, corporate reading of Psalms, offering words of praise and thanksgiving, etc. For more on worship in small group, visit: vcsmallgroups.org/h-o-s-t-training-videos/ Click the video "HOST Training: Worship & Prayer"

Watch the Video and Fill In Teaching Outline (20 minutes)

Discussion Questions (30 minutes): The HOST can ask the provided question and encourage everyone to participate and share their thoughts. Each group will vary in its personality and flow. Feel free to omit or modify questions as you see fit.

Prayer Ministry Time (15-20 minutes): In the Vineyard, we don't just want to talk about things—we want the things we talk about to affect change in our lives. So, we take some time at the end of each session to process what we've learned and discussed through prayer. We call this time "prayer ministry time." The guide gives a suggestion for each week. This is not just a time to process, but it's really a time to experience God. God is alive and active among his creation. The Prayer Ministry Time in the discussion guide portion of this workbook is meant to be a time to reflect and connect with God. We believe in listening for God to speak privately through prayer and listening for God to speak in the presence of others. This is a mystery, but with practice there will be increasing clarity in hearing God's voice together. Beyond what is written for each week, here are two additional options for prayer ministry time:

1. In groups of 2 or 3 ask if there is anything in each other's lives that you need prayer for. Pray a prayer of encouragement that asks God to meet them in their need.

2. If you have been trained to listen to God in a corporate setting either in Leadership Training 2 or through our Meeting God 301 class, then please implement this practice into your Prayer Ministry Time with your group.

TIPS FOR A GREAT SMALL GROUP

Being in a small group can be intimidating. Most people, especially first-timers, aren't comfortable sharing what they're going through with others. No matter your starting point, a healthy small group is consistently growing in trust, care, and even friendship. Here are a few tips to help move your group toward being a healthy, thriving group.

- Be friendly and be yourself. God wants to use you in your group through your unique gifts, personality, and experiences. So be the real you with your strengths and weaknesses—don't try to be anyone else!

- Silence is okay. When a question is asked, don't feel like you need to be the first person to jump in with an answer. Be aware of those who are quieter and give them an opportunity to share. People who like to take time before they speak may wait up to 30 seconds before they say something. Waiting in silence may feel awkward at first, but it will pay off!

- Pray for the other members of your group throughout the week. This is a good practice that all members should eventually be encouraged to do. A group email or Facebook group may help group members to remember to pray for each other and to share prayer requests throughout the week.

- Share responsibility for your group. You may have signed up to be the HOST and had some initial leadership training, but each person can play a part. Some may want to help with the snack, while others might want to help lead discussion or even lead a time of worship at the beginning of the meeting. John Wimber, the founder of the Vineyard movement, loved to say, "Everybody gets to play!" Try to find a way that each person can play a role.

- Don't worry about finishing all the questions. What's most important is that you connect as a group to see what God is doing in each of your lives and how you can support each other through life's ups and downs. A great way to facilitate discussion is to be familiar with the questions ahead of time, and even have some of your own answers in mind in case no one else shares. This can also be a great way to decide in advance which questions to skip in case time becomes a factor.

THE REAL JESUS

WEEK 1

THE JESUS OF HISTORY

THE REAL JESUS

GETTING STARTED

To start, go around the room and have each person share their name and answer these two questions: How did you get involved in this group? What do you hope to get out of this series?

TEACHING OUTLINE

Reasons for Doubt

- We may doubt because of ___family Background___.

- We may doubt because of the bad behavior of ___other Christians___.

- We may have doubts because we compare ___our strong___ faith with the faith of ___the weak believers / others___.

"'If you can?' said Jesus. 'Everything is possible for one who believes.' Immediately the boy's father exclaimed, 'I do believe; help me overcome my unbelief!'" - Mark 9:23-24

Evidence for Belief

- The testimony of the ___Roman___ government.

"The beginning of the good news about Jesus the Messiah…" - Mark 1:1a

- The testimony of ___eyewitnesses of Jesus / truth of knowledge___ regarding Jesus.

"A certain man from Cyrene, Simon, the father of Alexander and Rufus, was passing by on his way in from the country, and they forced him to carry the cross." - Mark 15:21

- The testimonies regarding Jesus include ___embarrassing personal experience / embarrassing material___ material.

THE JESUS OF HISTORY

DISCUSSION QUESTIONS

If someone had never met you directly, what are ways they could still get to know you?

Have you ever doubted Jesus was who the Bible says he is? What caused these doubts or questions?

Do you find the video's evidence for belief that Jesus existed as a human compelling? What stood out as credible? What do you still have questions about?

Has your understanding of who Jesus is changed over the past decade? How about since you were a child?

Are there other people that have positively or negatively shaped the way you view who Jesus is? How?

THE REAL JESUS

PRAYER MINISTRY TIME

For some of you, this may feel awkward. It will be important to cultivate this time – don't skip this part of the study! There's something that happens as we pray and we invite God's presence in that gives perspective and allows space for God to meet us in positive and sometimes surprising ways (if necessary, go back and review the section on Prayer Ministry Time in the "How to Use this Workbook" section above).

We want to take a few moments to be honest about our doubts and also ask God to reveal places where he might have been present in our lives. So, let's get started!

The HOST will start by saying these simple words: "Holy Spirit, come. We invite you here. We want to know and experience the real Jesus." Then, just wait for a few moments (20 seconds or so).

Everyone has doubts, and it is okay to acknowledge your doubts. Take a minute and, in the space provided below, write down doubts you might have about the real Jesus. Is it related to past experiences with your family? Your experience in the church or with Christians? Do you doubt because you went through a hard experience in your life? Some of us have a long list of doubts. Write down whatever comes to mind. We've already invited God into these moments; let God guide you.

    Doubts:

After a minute (or so), pray these words, "Jesus, I want to believe that you are real, but help me in my unbelief."

Now, in the space provided below, write down places where something good happened in your life. Did you ever have an experience when you were younger when you felt the love and presence of Jesus and you miss it? Have you ever been given an opportunity that you weren't qualified for or deserved? What did that feel like? Where was God in these experiences?

     Evidences:

After a brief time, pray these words, "sometimes we overlook evidence in our own lives of where you have been really good to us Jesus. Help us not miss you in this journey."
The HOST will close out your time in prayer of thanks.

NOTES AND REFLECTIONS

NOTES AND REFLECTIONS

THE REAL JESUS

DAY 1: ARE YOU FOR REAL?

MARK 1:1-20 WITH A FOCUS ON 1:16-20

Who is the real Jesus? Your answer today will probably be different than the one you give 40 days from now – at the conclusion of this series – and that's a good thing! In fact, we see this evolution of understanding modeled in the lives of the very first people to follow Jesus: his disciples. Even they didn't always get it right.

The Gospel of Mark zooms quickly right out of the gate. Unlike the other gospels, which provide more backstory in their opening verses, here in Mark, Jesus is calling his first disciples before the first chapter even ends. He's about to go public with his rescue plan! When looking at verses 16-20 closer, try to imagine in your mind's eye a little more dialogue: as Jesus calls these men, their first response is, "Are you serious?" Surely, some of them were at least thinking, "Come on Jesus, you want me to leave behind the entire life I know, 'without delay,' and follow you? Why are you singling me out? Are you for real? You may be the Messiah, the one God promised to send, but how can I be sure?"

Throughout Mark, which we will read in its entirety, Jesus is going to keep doing, saying, and demanding things that will leave the disciples, and us the readers, asking, "Are you for real?" This question makes sense because there has never been nor will there ever be anyone like Jesus. Go with it. Jesus welcomes your inquiry and lovingly invites you into this journey to discover who he really is.

THE REAL JESUS

Take a few moments to sit quietly and write a short list of questions – perhaps three to five – that you have about the person of Jesus. Over the next 40 days, as you continue with these devotionals, and watch and discuss the videos in your small group, refer back to these questions. Perhaps you'll get some answers. Or maybe you'll realize that you've asked the wrong questions. Which is totally OK! Remember, this is a time to fine tune your understanding of who Jesus is and to inch your heart, mind, and soul closer to him.

DIGGING DEEPER

What opportunities do you have to be a better disciple to more closely follow Jesus in thought, word, and deed? Maybe you're holding on to something – not a sin, but something good, like the disciples' fishing business – because you're afraid. Giving it to Jesus to do with it as he wills seems too great a cost. Or maybe you see discipleship as something that doesn't require consistent faithfulness; it's more like a hat you can put on and take off, according to your desires. Perhaps it's as straightforward as your actions missing the mark: you gossip, you drink too much, or you don't have active compassion for the poor. Talk to the Lord about any shortcomings that come to mind. Ask him to highlight one of them and reveal some ways to change and grow as a disciple. Pray for grace to walk it out.

THE REAL JESUS

DAY 2: A FORETASTE

MARK 1:21--2:12 WITH A FOCUS ON 1:40-45

Have you ever attended a long, formal wedding ceremony? Perhaps by the time the food was served you realized you weren't in the best mood. Some call this being "hangry," full of hunger-fueled anger. That's not a feeling you want to have at a joyous celebration!

Here's the wonderful thing about Jesus: he doesn't make us wait in hunger and desperation. Freely, he gives us what we need. In today's scripture, we see that the crowds – everyday people like you and me – are quickly figuring out that there's something wonderful and exceptional about Jesus. The Good News is spreading! Most Bibles break down the different sections of this chunk of scripture with these titles: Jesus Drives Out an Impure Spirit, Jesus Heals Many, Jesus Heals a Man with Leprosy, and Jesus Forgives and Heals a Paralyzed Man. What is so wonderfully different about Jesus? What is he serving? Divine healing! And lots of it!

In heaven, where God's rule and reign saturate 100% of everything, there is no sickness, disease, or death. As part of Jesus' earthly ministry, he serves heavenly appetizers of healing; he blesses the people with a taste of God's Kingdom. The real Jesus inaugurates the reality of God's Kingdom: his reign on earth. Verses 1:40-45 clue us into more of what's motivating Jesus. He heals because he has compassion on us. He heals us because it's what he wants to do.

We'll take a closer look at Jesus the healer in week three of this series, but for now, let's focus on the leprous man's transformative faith. In verse 40, we see he knows Jesus can heal him, but he's just not sure it's something Jesus wants to do. Then, in verse 45, after he's healed, the man is so excited that he defies Jesus' command to keep quiet about it.

Perhaps you can relate to the man as seen in verse 40 and are reluctant to believe God has compassion for you. This disbelief could pertain to anything: a need for healing, a feeling that your mistakes have placed you beyond the reach of God's love, a tendency to hold God's compassion at arm's length because you'd rather earn his acceptance, etc. Write down your thoughts as a prayer to God, asking him for a foretaste of his Kingdom. If you see yourself more on the other side, believing fully in God's compassion for you, take a moment to ask God for opportunities to share freely about all that he has done for you. Pray this would draw people closer to the real Jesus.

DIGGING DEEPER

Within these passages, mostly about healing, we find one seemingly off-topic section: verses 1:35-39. In the midst of healing many people, Jesus gets up very early in the morning to pray. Showing people what God's Kingdom is all about – by healing the sick, setting captives free, bringing Good News to the poor, etc. – can take a lot out of you. It's worth it, but it's exhausting! Jesus regularly reenergized by spending time alone with his Heavenly Father.

What time and space do you create in your life to meet with God and allow him to fill you with his love and power? Open your hands to God and say: "Speak, Lord, for your servant is listening." Then, just sit in silence. Don't strain to try and hear God's voice. He will speak if he wants to. Receive this simple act of stillness and silence as a gift package of replenishment.

THE REAL JESUS

DAY 3: GOOD GONE BAD

MARK 2:13--3:6 WITH A FOCUS ON 2:23-28

Leave it to my three-year-old to ruin a good thing. She resists bedtime, something that is for her good (and my sanity!); she refuses to eat many healthy foods. Even treats can become a tragedy if they aren't served according to her very particular whims. Truthfully, this is something all of humanity is prone to do. What God intends for our good, we have a tendency to spoil.

The Pharisees, highly respected religious experts of Jesus' day, were known for strict adherence to the requirements of the laws given to them by Moses in the Old Testament. But often, they took it to an extreme that was never part of God's good intention for the law. He designed the law to protect his people and to provide a way to live at peace with themselves, with others, and with God.

By focusing more heavily on protecting the law instead of living to please God, the Pharisees took a good thing and ruined it. This is why Jesus was always on their radar; they didn't like the way he observed – or in their view, failed to observe – Jewish law. They jumped at any chance to accuse him of breaking a religious rule.

In today's passage, the Pharisees insist that by failing to fast, Jesus broke the Sabbath. They are missing the bigger, more important picture. Reminding them of King David's actions from long ago, Jesus is saying the long awaited king, the one which fasting and other religious observations pointed to, is here. And Jesus is the king of everything, even the Sabbath. Instead of receiving the good thing – Jesus as their king – the Pharisees were insisting he was a tragedy and called him bad.

God's rules are for our benefit. If you tend to think of God as someone waiting to call you out for breaking a rule instead of looking out for your best interest, what do you feel are contributors to this view of him? What God-given rules do you think of as burdensome? Perhaps some aspect of your temperament, upbringing, etc., adds burdens to God's perfect way of living. You may be carrying around rules and expectations that he never intended for us to carry. Ask God to speak about his good intentions for you. Wait in silence for one minute, then journal a response to him.

DIGGING DEEPER

Re-read Mark 3:1-6, the last section of today's readings. On the Sabbath, even an objectively good thing like divine healing was deemed off-limits to them. The Pharisees were hyper-focused on Sabbath observance because they believed it was a critically important part of their identity – something that set them apart from the pagans in their midst – and a pointer to the ultimate rest they'd get when God freed them from their political oppressors. In this way, they don't sound far from God's heart, right?

In what ways have you celebrated the Sabbath well? When have you failed to experience its goodness? Today, it's less about the tyranny of legalistic rules and more about our overstuffed "always on" lives. What we pack into every other day of the week – work, exercise, shopping, errands, screentime, chores, etc. – are often the same things we pack into the one day God calls us to rest and recenter. What is at least one thing you can designate as off-limits on the Sabbath? How might this bring you closer to the real Jesus?

DAY 4: WHO DO YOU THINK YOU ARE?

MARK 3:7-35 WITH A FOCUS ON 3:20-35

Family members often have a gift for pigeonholing. There's an aunt who still sees you as a small child and pinches your cheek at every family gathering. During holidays with extended family, the same stories of you are told over and over, as if you've never changed. I have a friend who once told his mother-in-law he really likes raspberries. Since then, his birthday celebrations have one dominant theme: raspberries. Raspberry candy, raspberry jam, raspberry ice cream, raspberry cake. To his mother-in-law, he is first and foremost a raspberry fanatic.

A question posed by Pastor Rich at the beginning of this week's video touches on this very subject. If someone was to get to know the real you, what do you think the best way would be to go about it? If they relied only on your family-of-origin, their perception of you may be skewed or over-simplified.

Jesus dealt with this in his own family. Mark 3:7-19 tells us that while the crowds were still wild about him and he continued to gather followers, his family wasn't having any of it. Verse 3:21 says, "...they went to take charge of him, for they said, 'He is out of his mind.'" Sometimes, when you do what God is calling you to do, it flies in the face of your family's long-held perception of you. In 3:22 the religious leaders go so far as to say he is possessed by Satan. Jesus was turning everything they held dear – their priorities and values – upside down. Surely, they thought, evil must be afoot!

THE REAL JESUS

This passage may press a few of your buttons, good and bad. Maybe you have an affinity for Jesus because you also feel misunderstood by others. Or perhaps, upon honest reflection, you can count yourself among those who misunderstand Jesus and his capabilities. Do glimpses of the real Jesus challenge any of your long-held assumptions and values? What new outlook do you sense Jesus offering to you? How does this make you feel? Anxious? Upset? Resistant? Excited? Journal through your thoughts.

DIGGING DEEPER

Re-read what Jesus says to both the experts and his family in Mark 3:23-35. Difficult passages such as this provide an opportunity to clear up misunderstandings of Jesus.

In verses 23-30 Jesus told the scribes that he is the stronger one. He demonstrates it by his power over Satan and all other evil forces. This should be Good News to everyone, religious leaders included, but they refuse to see it. They have pigeonholed Jesus as an enemy. That leads us to Jesus' harsh words in verses 28-29. Anyone who sees the work of the Holy Spirit and insists it's the work of the Devil has crossed a permanent line into territory that blinds one to the truth.

In verses 31-35, Jesus confronted the cultural value of family loyalty. He is shocking his family of origin and the culture at large by starting a new family, one made up of his followers instead of blood relatives. It's both simple and revolutionary.

Sit with these sobering verses for a few minutes and take some time to pray loyalty to Jesus would surpass pledges you've made to anyone or anything else.

DAY 5: STORYTIME 101

MARK 4:1-20

Some of the best stories are the ones that show you a glimpse of yourself, those that subtly compel you to do some soul-searching. Jesus was really good at telling stories like this. In fact, storytelling was his main way of teaching people what God and his Kingdom were all about. And it gave his audience members a chance to think about where they may fit into God's story.

In The Parable of the Sower, Jesus uses farming imagery – something easily understood by his listeners – to describe the different responses one can have to hearing about the Good News of God's Kingdom coming to earth.

Instead of painting a picture of different types of soil, Jesus could've just said, "Hey, scribes: your hearts are so hard that you're never going to get the point. Plain and simple. As for all of you in the crowd: you may be excited about the message now, because I'm healing you and casting demons out of you, but your enthusiasm is gonna wane when hard times inevitably come. And Mom, I'm sorry to say this, but the noise of your worried thoughts about me bucking tradition is preventing you from being able to hear about how I've come to set you and all people free." But that's not a story. It doesn't invite people in. It's a list of accusations; one so blunt and offensive that it could've been the end of Jesus' public ministry right then and there.

Jesus takes another route; he uses story and rich imagery to compel the audience to look within. The Kingdom of God is a divine mystery. One of the ways it seeps into our souls is via story.

As we conclude this first week of investigating the real Jesus, what sort of story do you see for your life? What chapter are you in? Where do you see yourself going? As for this specific parable, try to determine which type of soil reflects the condition of your heart. What do you think God wants you to do with this revelation? Going forward, pray he'd use symbols and imagery that deeply resonate and bring about change in your life. Ask God that you would be "ever perceiving" and "ever understanding" whenever he tells you a story.

DIGGING DEEPER

Focus on Mark 4:8. Good soil holds moisture and nutrients in perfect balance so that plants can thrive and produce an abundant crop. Good spiritual soil means that your heart is open to and understanding of Jesus' message. As Rich shared in this week's video, openness to the real Jesus means you are not closed off by rigid thinking, family background, or the poor behavior of Christians.

Just like a farmer can amend bad soil to make it good, so can our hearts transform to be more open to and rooted in the real Jesus. This is part of what makes conversion an ongoing process. Philippians 1:6 says, "...he who began a good work in you will carry it on to completion..." Picture your heart as a plot of ground needing to be regularly tended and amended. What might Jesus the divine farmer amend and improve in you today? Your outlook on a relationship? A sense of hope? Your commitment to loving your kids or a friend? Ask Jesus to transform your heart. Don't settle for static spirituality and don't try to change on your own. Today, throughout this series and beyond, let God nourish your heart and root you in him.

NOTES AND REFLECTIONS

NOTES AND REFLECTIONS

THE REAL JESUS

WEEK 2

JESUS THE TEACHER

THE REAL JESUS

GETTING STARTED

Go around the room and have each person share their name and who their favorite teacher was and what made that teacher so special.

TEACHING OUTLINE

"Again Jesus began to teach by the lake. The crowd that gathered around him was so large that he got into a boat and sat in it out on the lake, while all the people were along the shore at the water's edge." - Mark 4:1

"When he was alone, the Twelve and the others around him asked him about the parables. He told them, "The secret of the kingdom of God has been given to you. But to those on the outside everything is said in parables so that, 'they may be ever seeing but never perceiving, and ever hearing but never understanding; otherwise they might turn and be forgiven!'" - Mark 4:10-12

"Listen! A farmer went out to sow his seed. As he was scattering the seed, some fell along the path, and the birds came and ate it up. Some fell on rocky places, where it did not have much soil. It sprang up quickly, because the soil was shallow. But when the sun came up, the plants were scorched, and they withered because they had no root. Other seed fell among thorns, which grew up and choked the plants, so that they did not bear grain. Still other seed fell on good soil. It came up, grew and produced a crop, some multiplying thirty, some sixty, some a hundred times." - Mark 4:3-8

THE REAL JESUS

Jesus teaches about:

- The __HARD__ heart. Holding truth at arms length.

"The farmer sows the word. Some people are like seed along the path, where the word is sown. As soon as they hear it, Satan comes and takes away the word that was sown in them." - Mark 4:14-15

- The __SHALLOW__ heart. Never considering the implications of Jesus' teaching.

"Others, like seed sown on rocky places, hear the word and at once receive it with joy. But since they have no root, they last only a short time. When trouble or persecution comes because of the word, they quickly fall away." - Mark 4:16-17

- The __CROWED__ heart. Too many competing commitments.

"Still others, like seed sown among thorns, hear the word; but the worries of this life, the deceitfulness of wealth and the desires for other things come in and choke the word, making it unfruitful." - Mark 4:18-19

- The __GOOD__ heart. Allows Jesus to manage their lives.

"Others, like seed sown on good soil, hear the word, accept it, and produce a crop—some thirty, some sixty, some a hundred times what was sown." - Mark 4:20

THE REAL JESUS

DISCUSSION QUESTIONS

Do you find yourself asking about the larger question of life's meaning and the "big questions" mentioned in the video or do you prefer to keep life more simple? Why do you think you are this way?

Do you find your primary view of Jesus is as a teacher or as a different role? What contributed to you viewing Jesus primarily in this role?

Does talking about the purpose of life or God bring you anxiety, exhaustion, boredom, excitement?

Have there been any significant lessons that you have applied in your life because of Jesus? How did it turn out for you?

Of the four types, in which state do you find your heart presently toward a relationship with Jesus? Hard, Shallow, Crowded, Good.

PRAYER MINISTRY TIME

The HOST will start by saying these simple words: "Holy Spirit, come. We invite you here. We want to know and experience the real Jesus." Then, just like last week, wait for a few moments (30 seconds or so).

Take a few minutes and relax and reflect on what you heard in the video. Ask yourself what kind of soil am I right now? Ask God to show you places where your heart might be hard and unwilling to listen to Jesus' lessons in your life right now. Is it in a relationship? A work situation?

Ask God to reveal places where you feel shallow right now – places where you're unwilling to let Jesus and others beneath the surface of your life.

Where does your life feel too crowded and busy? Has work become so oppressive that you've lost sight of family or other friendships? Where are you pushing relationships out of your life?

Pair up with someone in your group and share your thoughts. Have them pray for you and ask God to help "work the soil" of your heart this week.

THE REAL JESUS
NOTES AND REFLECTIONS

NOTES AND REFLECTIONS

THE REAL JESUS

DAY 1: IF YOU LISTEN, YOU CAN HEAR

MARK 4:21-34 WITH A FOCUS ON 4:21-25

Sometimes, paying close attention is of utmost importance. If an apprentice working under a master mechanic isn't fully engaged in learning the correct way to fix cars – let's say he daydreams while on the job or never reviews material he's already learned – not only will he be less competitive in the job market, but he may also make mistakes that put people's lives in danger. Or imagine taking a CPR class and instead of paying close attention you find yourself reading articles and scrolling social media. Would you be able to help someone who went into cardiac arrest?

What makes it possible to really learn something and really retain the information in a way that makes a difference in your life? You may pay close attention to your instructor, set all distractions aside, take notes, practice what you've been taught, ask the instructor follow-up questions, etc. This is the posture Jesus wants us to take when he teaches us. <u>Understanding the Kingdom of God requires a high level of attentiveness</u>. And since following Jesus doesn't happen in a sterile classroom, <u>we learn from him in the richness of real life</u>. We read, "With the measure you use, it will be measured to you – and even more." In other words, don't just learn it – live it.

Whenever Jesus taught, there were probably varying levels of attentiveness among those in the crowd. "If anyone has ears to hear, let them hear." The ears of some surely perked up, as though they were hearing great authority and challenge and answers to prayer for the first time in their life. They were ready to put his words into practice. Others were likely distracted, cynical, or skeptical.

THE REAL JESUS

Consider how you relate to Jesus as a teacher. Do you lean in, paying close attention, believing he's the smartest person ever? Or are you distracted by your wandering mind, the birds outside the window, your to-do list, etc.? Are you both a student and a practitioner? Jesus wants his teaching to be both learned and lived; do you embody this? Take a moment to pray that for the remainder of this series, your time attending small group, listening to sermons, participating in the service project, and doing the devotionals would be a season of profound learning. If you sense God speaking any "here's how to live it" advice to you, jot it down.

DIGGING DEEPER

Scientific understanding of learning has greatly evolved the past 50 years. School is not the only place to acquire knowledge. Nor is the workplace the only setting where you can apply what you know. Learning can happen in all environments, at all stages of life. This new understanding is what we call "lifelong learning."

Think about whether you are a spiritual lifelong learner. Over the course of following Jesus, how teachable have you been? In every season of life, are you his student, sitting at his feet, as disciples of Rabbis did in that day? Take some time to journal about your journey as a lifelong learner of Jesus: What did you once believe about Jesus and his mission for the world that you now know to be misguided? What did you use to think was "bad"? What was "good"? How is the Lord working on you now; what's going on in your heart and mind that he wants to change? Thank God for the opportunity to be a lifelong learner of Jesus and pray you will always be teachable.

THE REAL JESUS

DAY 2: POWER STRUGGLE

MARK 4:35-41

"I have the power!" If you're an American child of the 1980s, this needs no explanation. For those not familiar with this catchphrase, a bit of backstory: He-Man and the Masters of the Universe was a Saturday morning cartoon set on the planet Eternia. Whenever main character Prince Adam holds his sword in the air and proclaims, "By the power of Grayskull...I have the power!" he magically transforms into He-Man, the most powerful man in the universe. Together with his allies, he uses this power to fight the bad guys.

Power is a major theme in the gospel of Mark. Each eyewitness account of Jesus' life has a certain audience in mind. For Mark, it's non-Jews called Gentiles; specifically, Roman soldiers. If anyone in ancient Israel represented institutionalized power, it was the Roman soldier, a ubiquitous reminder of Rome's occupation and oppression of the Jewish homeland.

Meanwhile, power also mattered to the Jewish hearers of this message. Eager for the long-awaited Messiah to powerfully overthrow an oppressive regime, they also recognized power in things like the sea. Throughout scripture, it represents chaotic and evil power. And yet, here's Jesus, rebuking a storm at sea. In verse 41, the disciples proclaim, "Who is this? Even the wind and the waves obey him!" He's no longer just a gifted teacher. He is a powerful King who has dominion over even nature. He is the king of everything. He has the power!

As Mark makes the case for Jesus' absolute power, perhaps there are situations in your life that cause you to doubt this assertion. When the disciples woke Jesus up during the storm, they were probably hoping he would call out to God to overpower the evil forces on the sea. They weren't expecting a tremendous display of power directly from him. What do you expect from Jesus? Can he miraculously overpower your cancer diagnosis or mental illness? Can he calm the storm of marital betrayal?

YES HE CAN, if it is HIS will

DEVOTIONALS FOR JESUS THE TEACHER

Generational poverty? The devastation of disasters, both natural and manmade? A loved one's addiction? Write down a few circumstances in your life where you need Jesus' power to overcome darkness and chaos. What would it look like for his power to invade the situation? Over the course of this week, pray for God's power to calm your life's storms.

DIGGING DEEPER

Reflect on verse 40 and the role of faith. How much does faith in God's presence and power matter? What does faith look like? Is Jesus the model of faith here – so confident in God's protection that he can sleep through a violent storm? Is this the real Jesus showing us real faith? Or does his behavior point to something more?

At the crucifixion, Jesus is not asleep on a boat, but nailed to a cross. His questions fit here, too: "Why are you so afraid? Do you still have no faith?" Imagine the disciples asking themselves these questions as they watch their beloved Lord die. They didn't know that just as Jesus defeated the evil of the storm, he would soon defeat all evil, even death. They were probably completely faithless at the crucifixion. And then thrilled, but still confused, when they found the tomb empty. And yet, despite their confusion and lack of faith, Jesus still rose from the dead. Ask God to overpower your own faithlessness and confusion.

THE REAL JESUS

DAY 3: LEGION OF DOOM

MARK 5:1-20

The Gospel of Mark feels as action-packed as a J.R.R. Tolkien novel. Jesus and the disciples go from one adventure to another, at an exhausting pace. Recall what happened immediately before Mark 5: Jesus and his disciples just survived a furious storm at sea, in the middle of the night. The disciples were likely on edge. And now here they are in Gerasenes, non-Jewish territory known for worship of evil gods, at a graveyard in the dark of night. A demonized man, full of superhuman strength, runs up to them, as he cries out and cuts himself. What a nightmare! They probably wanted to catch up on all the sleep the storm had robbed, but instead they are confronted by a legion of demons determined to destroy someone's life. They just found out Jesus had power over nature. But does he have power over demons, especially so many ferocious ones?

Satan is out to destroy. He wants us to lose everything: morality, relationships, dignity, health, sanity, livelihood, etc. Just look at how much the legion of demons took away from this one man. Jesus and his Kingdom are the opposite; he is infinitely good and out to restore, with power. Here, Jesus demonstrates his power over evil by sending the demons into a large herd of pigs. What a sight that must've been! It's like an epic scene from The Lord of the Rings.

The restored man was totally on board with Jesus' agenda and ready to tell the whole world about it, but one wonders what the exhausted disciples must've felt. Was the constant drama all just too weird? Too scary? Too intense? Maybe simply reading this story has you feeling similarly. In the 21st century, to consider demonization as a possible explanation for someone's affliction places you in an extreme minority. Yet, in every ancient account of Jesus' life, from both ancient historians and the Bible, Jesus was recognized as someone who encountered and had power over evil spirits.

Journal some of your thoughts, hesitations, fears, and questions about demonic oppression. Consider this a prayer to Jesus. What do you sense him speaking in return?

DIGGING DEEPER

Let's talk about the community's response to the demon-possessed man's restoration. Re-read Mark 5:14-17. They didn't join the man in celebrating his newfound freedom from oppression. If setting people free and experiencing other tastes of God's Kingdom here on earth meant losing money, they were out. Jesus and his life-giving mission weren't welcome in their town.

Whether the cause is spiritual or otherwise, are there things that prevent you from welcoming Jesus' Kingdom into your life and the lives of others? Perhaps it's something that would involve too much sacrifice or is too inconvenient. Say there's an addict in your family. You don't pray for her recovery because that would likely mean more interaction with her, and that could be messy. Maybe you allow ambition to climb the ladder at work to supersede what God wants you to prioritize: improving workplace ethics, developing relationships with co-workers, etc. Tell God you're sorry for avoiding his mission. Pray for a changed heart, and that you'd be filled with grace and courage to partner with Jesus in Kingdom ministry, no matter the cost.

THE REAL JESUS

DAY 4: FREEDOM IN FAITH

MARK 5:21-34 WITH A FOCUS ON 5:25-34

While not edible, there's something in today's passage called a "Markan sandwich." A few times in the gospel of Mark, like the filling between two pieces of bread, you find a story within a story. Today's inside story is that of a sick woman driven to desperation. Her constant bleeding meant she'd been ceremonially unclean for 12 years. She had spent most of her money on ineffective medical care and became relationally and emotionally bankrupt due to years of avoiding others out of fear of making them unclean. This is why she approached Jesus in fear: she didn't want him to know she touched him, and she didn't want anyone else in the crowd to realize an unclean person was among them. But fear didn't stop her from pursuing freedom; she "did it afraid." By secretly touching Jesus, she's healed! Let's tally the score: so far we know that Jesus has power over the natural world, evil, and now sickness. And, if you think about it, he even has power over our fears.

Where does your fear take you? Do you mix it in with faith to concoct a willingness to take risks? Or does fear hem you in, restraining your growth and preventing your freedom? New Testament scholar N.T. Wright highlights the relationship between fear and faith: "...there is still room for us to creep up behind Jesus – if that's all we feel we can do – and reach out and touch him, in that odd mixture of fear and faith that characterizes so much Christian discipleship... faith, though itself powerless, is that channel through which Jesus' power can work... and faith, however much fear and trembling may accompany it, is the first sign of that remaking, that renewal, that new life."

THE REAL JESUS

All of us have things we're afraid of. What role will you allow the real Jesus to play in your fears? In examining Mark's many accounts of Jesus' power, maybe you feel this testimony doesn't line up with your experience of the many fearful and overwhelming things you face. You may wonder if Jesus has either forgotten you or is unwilling to demonstrate his power in your life. Lift your fears up to God. Pray this act would give rise to a faith that channels God's power and gives you renewed confidence in his care for you. This week, what is one way you can step out in this bolstered faith?

DIGGING DEEPER

In the bread slices of this sandwich story, Mark introduces us to Jesus' most tremendous display of power: authority over death. Jairus, one of the synagogue leaders of this small town, would probably prefer to avoid messy, rule-breaking Jesus, but he was desperate; his daughter was dying! Both he and the hemorrhaging woman were completely spent – willing to do whatever it takes to get what they needed.

All of us have been there: emotionally, physically, financially, or relationally spent. In what ways is Jesus inviting you to welcome his power into these times? The people in verse 35 seem to take a "why bother?" position. We can be a different kind of people! We can pray for the sick, relieve the burdened, speak freedom to the traumatized, pursue restoration of a relationship, and pray for someone's radical conversion. The real Jesus is with you!

THE REAL JESUS

DAY 5: HOMEGROWN MARGINALIZATION

MARK 6:1-13 WITH A FOCUS ON 6:1-6

For better or for worse, society and culture expects certain things of certain people. When it's "for worse," people are limited in their ability to experience life to the full – they are boxed in by rigid, oppressive, or unreasonable expectations. This harms individuals, but it's also a loss for society when they can't make their mark the way God intends.

Historically, many people have held the belief that women aren't cut out for careers in STEM (science, technology, engineering, and math). However, several women's lives testify otherwise. Marie Curie's work in radioactivity twice won her the Nobel Prize in the early 1900s, long before the last century's many strides toward gender equality. The film Hidden Figures chronicles the true story of Katherine Globe Johnson, Dorothy Vaughan, and Mary Jackson, African-American scientists who made significant contributions to the Space Race in the 1960s. Most recently, in November 2017, Canadian PhD student Caitlin Miron made a groundbreaking discovery that may be able to stop cancer cells from spreading. That these individuals are exceptions to the rule is not because of a general lack of ability among women. Rather, studies show women are often steered away from careers in STEM due to factors like teasing in school, a lack of encouragement, stereotypes, and bias. When society blocks women's paths to STEM fields, it's to our detriment.

When oppressed and hemmed in, people may seek a refuge, a place that is more tolerant and encouraging of breaking the mold. You'd think that going back home, to surround yourself with people who know you well, would be such a place. Whenever Jesus returned to his hometown, this was not the case. He endured belittling and judgment everywhere he went, it seems.

THE REAL JESUS

In Mark 6:1-6, as in Mark 3:20-35, obedience to God – fulfilling his purpose – offended those in his hometown. Believing him to be nothing more than a hometown boy of illegitimate birth, they didn't ask for healing. He was no miracle-worker in their eyes. Instead of accepting all he was capable of, people probably leered at Jesus, thinking the worst of him. As a result, they missed out on experiencing God's best for them.

Limited and misguided thinking about Jesus persists today. But it certainly doesn't stop with him. As we try to take hold of the real Jesus during this series, we can also affirm the realness of others. Consider the different people you interact with: children, the opposite sex, people of races and ethnic backgrounds different than your own, those who aren't neurotypical, etc. Pick one such group and spend the next day being mindful of your interactions. Ask God to show you the full humanity and capability he sees in each person.

DIGGING DEEPER

How can we clear away whatever clouds our spiritual eyesight in order to truly see the real Jesus and receive all he wants to offer us? Try this visualization exercise: close your eyes; unlike those in Nazareth, warmly welcome the person of Jesus into your home, your territory. Picture him walking toward you. Instead of amazing Jesus with a lack of faith, amaze him with a heart full of faith. Don't put labels and preconceived notions on him. Allow him to flood your life with the good news of the Kingdom. What do you see? What do you hear? How do you feel? Journal a response to God.

THE REAL JESUS
NOTES AND REFLECTIONS

NOTES AND REFLECTIONS

THE REAL JESUS

WEEK 3

JESUS THE HEALER

THE REAL JESUS

GETTING STARTED

Go around the room, share your name and answer these questions: What is the first thing that comes to your mind when you hear the word "healer"? What people do you typically think of when you think of praying for healing?

TEACHING OUTLINE

"As soon as they left the synagogue, they went with James and John to the home of Simon and Andrew. Simon's mother-in-law was in bed with a fever, and they immediately told Jesus about her. So he went to her, took her hand and helped her up. The fever left her and she began to wait on them." - Mark 1:29-31

- Jesus' healings were not a matter of **Hype**.

- Jesus' healings were not a matter of **religion**.

- Jesus' healings were not a matter of **Technique**.

- Jesus' healings are a matter of **the Love of God**.

"That evening after sunset the people brought to Jesus all the sick and demon-possessed. The whole town gathered at the door, and Jesus healed many who had various diseases. He also drove out many demons, but he would not let the demons speak because they knew who he was." - Mark 1:32-34

- Jesus, the healer, is **available**.

THE REAL JESUS

DISCUSSION QUESTIONS

Have you or anyone you've met claimed to have been healed by God? What was the event/experience?

Do you believe divine healing is possible? What contributes to your stance? *God can do anything if it is His Will*

How do you feel about offering to pray healing over someone outside of church? *CAREfully* If you have done this, describe what happened. Was it uncomfortable or weird? Was it comforting to the person?

Have you ever been surprised at the availability of Jesus? Maybe a time where you were experiencing consequences of your sin and shame and God surprised you with his love?

THE REAL JESUS

PRAYER MINISTRY TIME

As you heard on the video, Jesus is a healer and he is available to you today! We don't need to manufacture a spiritual or religious experience to find healing. We simply need God's presence. We need the real Jesus to show up! That's why we begin with these simple words of invitation. After you invite the Holy Spirit to come, give a longer pause to allow God to speak. In one of the stories shared in the video, one person received a specific word about a specific need for healing for someone else.

The HOST will pray these words: "Holy Spirit, come. We invite you here. We want to know and experience the real Jesus. Would you give us specific words or impressions about anyone in this room that might need healing right now?" At this point, take a couple minutes and just wait in the quiet. You've asked God to speak. Now, give him the opportunity to do so.

After this pause, the HOST will ask if anyone sensed a specific need for anyone in the room. Take a risk if you sensed Jesus speaking and share it. Someone might need to know God sees them, very much like Roxi (the woman mentioned in the video) needed to know God saw her! If there is something, pray as a group together for the person.

If not, that's OK, too! Break into two groups. If you have anything that needs healing, simply ask the group to pray for you. Take time to pray for healing for each other. Remember, Jesus is available in these moments!

NOTES AND REFLECTIONS

THE REAL JESUS
NOTES AND REFLECTIONS

NOTES AND REFLECTIONS

THE REAL JESUS

DAY 1: FAITHFUL AND OBEDIENT

MARK 6:14-44 WITH A FOCUS ON 6:30-44

In his Kingdom, we can count on Jesus to ask us to do things that seem beyond our capability. We don't just watch him bring the Kingdom to the hungry; he turns to us and says, "You give them something to eat." And so we do it – perhaps with a lack of belief in our own ability, like the disciples did in verse 37 of this text. But then it happens: a miracle. There's more than enough for everyone to eat because the disciples obediently passed out the food.

Miracles can come in small forms: a strained relationship becomes peaceful, you feel led to pay for the coffee of the person behind you in line. They can come in big forms: the baby is here because you pushed for two hours. You are freed from an addiction. Miracles of all types are expressions of God's extravagant love and provision. When the disciples picked up the abundant leftovers, it was Jesus' way of saying, "I care about you and I will provide for you to do what I ask of you, no matter how incapable you feel, no matter how limited the resources." Jesus asks us to have faith in his ability and his desire to work through us. While the day will come when God's Kingdom will be established in full, for now we embrace our role as miracle-doing heralds of its coming. When God wants to use you to perform a miracle, don't worry about your limitations. To paraphrase 1 Thessalonians 5:24, he is faithful, and he will do it.

THE REAL JESUS

What problems – personal, societal, etc. – seem impossible to fix? In those situations, could God be saying to you, as he said to the disciples, "You do it."? To follow Jesus is to have authority in doing the things he did. When he says, "You do it," we can and we should! Write down 2-3 of the "impossibles" that weigh on your heart, those things that seem beyond your ability to fix. Then, ask God to inspire you with one idea to actively tackle each issue. Visualize what it would look like for Jesus to show up as you walk in obedience. It may take a few minutes to sense what God is speaking; that's normal. This week, turn one of your inspirations into an action. Pray God would go ahead of you and pour out his extravagance.

DIGGING DEEPER

Mark is transitioning us from simply observing Jesus' tremendous displays of power to hitting us with a command: "You do it, too." While a Christ-like lifestyle often involves conventional means – speaking out against injustice, caring for orphans, being a good neighbor, etc. – here, and again in Mark 8 with another miraculous feeding of a multitude, Jesus is underlining our surprising capacity to do miracles as he did.

Consider whether you lean too heavily on conventional means of spreading the Good News. Do you neglect your miracle-making capabilities, the deeds Jesus so frequently modeled for us? Challenge yourself: for every conventional thing you do to bring God's kingdom to earth, ask him to show you a miracle you can do as well. As you step out in faith to do these miracles, keep this conversation going with the Lord and continually allow him to use you in astounding ways.

DAY 2: DOES NOT COMPUTE

MARK 6:45-56

Some of you may remember Y2K. If not, it's because computer scientists anticipated the problem and recoded computers across almost all software and systems before it happened. If they hadn't recoded anything, you would remember Y2K as the day computers died on earth.

If the disciples were computer systems, their software about the Messiah was flawed. It was coded to assume the anointed one would be a political leader who'd overthrow the oppressive Roman regime. There were no data fields insisting on the Messiah's rule over nature, sickness, etc. – nothing about his divinity. The data on him being the savior of the whole world, not just for Jews, was corrupted. Preconceived notions about Jesus are like buggy software in our faith system. You see this in Mark 6:48-52, especially verse 52. Despite all they'd seen Jesus do, they were still afraid and confused to see him walk on water. The truth of his messiahship coupled with his ultimate power and divinity did not compute. To put it another way: this version of Jesus as Messiah did not fit into their worldview.

Like a looming widespread computer crash, this completely upheaving and unthinkable truth about who Jesus really is has become a mounting tidal wave in the gospel of Mark. Will his disciples eventually surf along the wave, full of understanding about the real Jesus? Or will it crash over them, leaving them doubly confused?

THE REAL JESUS

Where do you find yourself: better understanding the real Jesus than you did a few weeks ago? Or struggling to compute everything about him? Journal an honest response to God, asking him to reprogram your assumptions about who Jesus is. Revisiting your questions from day one of this series may be helpful. Remember, God is incredibly patient with us in our journey toward understanding him. He warmly welcomes us when we vulnerably engage him along the way.

DIGGING DEEPER

In verse 50, Jesus says to the terrified disciples, "Take courage! It is I. Don't be afraid." The simple command, "Don't be afraid," is a frequent one in the Bible, occurring 365 times.

When we approach life from a place of fear, we think it's a protective measure, but it's really to our detriment. When we fear commitments like marriage or even making plans with someone, we miss out on valuable companionship. When we are afraid of people who are different from us – maybe they're from another country, speak a different language, or practice an unfamiliar religion – we forsake an opportunity to learn, grow, and simply be like Jesus to someone.

If every Christian let fear win, God's Kingdom would not go forth at any sort of measurable pace. What fears hound you? Hold them before the Lord and picture him saying directly to you, "Take courage! It is I." Imagine him holding courage out to you. In exchange for your fears, take it into your hands. What is the first thing you feel led to do with this courage? Make a plan to do so.

THE REAL JESUS

DAY 3: TREASURED TRADITION

MARK 7:1-23 WITH A FOCUS ON 7:6-15 AND 7:20-23

Holidays are rich with traditions. In America, some are observed en masse: come December, there's a Christmas tree in lots of windows; trick-or-treaters swarm the streets every Halloween. Then there are the ones specific to families: on Christmas Eve, you wear matching holiday-themed pajamas. Your family always sits in the same spot at the park to watch Independence Day fireworks. For other families, it's all about the food: Grandma always makes fudge at Christmas time. The Easter spread wouldn't be complete without your aunt's secret-recipe deviled eggs.

It's enjoyable to observe traditions – both your own and those of other families and cultures. But as much as we count on them to create a holiday vibe, are they law? Of course not. It's not appropriate to force your traditions on others or get really irritated when one doesn't unfold exactly how you want it to. Why? Because traditions are a means, not an end. They help orient us toward what really matters.

Tradition was something the Pharisees fiercely depended upon. To them, it seemed to be an end. They introduced many, many man-made rules and traditions in the hopes that the people would never even get close to breaking God's commands. You can't violate the decree to rest on the Sabbath – God's good rule – if you can't even put a log on the fire – a Pharisaical addendum. These verses in Mark 7 make it pretty clear that Jesus had no love for the Pharisees' add-ons. What does Jesus love? A heart transformed. This is the end we should pursue.

Jesus is the great transformer; the one who offers us so much more than external rearrangement. And yet, as he changes us on the inside, it does begin to show on the outside. How we approach everything in life begins to change. We relax our high expectations of holidays. We are above reproach in all of our interactions with the opposite sex. We admit when we're wrong.

We stop reading magazines and lifestyle blogs that spark envy in our hearts. When we truly understand the love God has for us, we focus less on looking the part or following all the rules. We aren't superficial; we aren't performance-oriented. Rather, out of the desire of our hearts we find ourselves living in the right relationship with God and others.

Where are you on this journey? In what ways are you holding loosely to the inconsequential and focusing instead on what matters to Jesus? What about the opposite? Pray for some insight and sit in silence for one minute, asking God to highlight aspects of your inner transformation. What can you celebrate? What is next?

DIGGING DEEPER

Our thoughts are like background music. Some songs nurture a sense of calm. Others incite negativity. Our thoughts, like music, are not benign. Jesus makes this pretty clear in verses 7:20-23.

Over the next week, keep a thought journal. Try to pen a few entries per day, especially when you're feeling moody, weak, judgmental, impatient, etc. This exercise will provide opportunities to both give thanks to God for pure and edifying thoughts – evidence of his transformational work – and express sorrow for the ways your thoughts miss the mark. Invite God to focus his transforming power on specific negative thoughts.

THE REAL JESUS

DAY 4: JESUS' SENSE OF HUMOR

MARK 7:24-8:13 WITH A FOCUS ON 7:24-30

If you can't take a joke, hanging out with Jesus may get a little awkward. In Mark 7, he basically calls a Gentile woman a dog. But with what tone of voice? What is his facial expression? His body language? It's off-base to envision this encounter playing out like orphan Oliver Twist fearfully asking Mr. Bumble for more. Rather, the exchange is much more playful and indicates that the woman is in on the joke; she "gets" Jesus. New Testament scholar N.T. Wright says she "accepts, after all, the apparent insult (Jews often thought of Gentiles as 'dogs,' and what Gentiles thought about Jews was usually just as uncomplimentary), and turns it to her own advantage."

But this is more than a woman's demonstration of faith wrapped up in a joke. There's also a political message here. Because it takes place with a Gentile woman in a Gentile town, Mark is showing us that Jesus' power over evil will go far beyond Jewish borders. Yes, Jesus is inaugurating God's Kingdom in Jewish territory, but ultimately he is the savior of the whole world!

Reflect on the title of this series: The Real Jesus: A Person Not a Religion. When we clear away the ceremony of religion, we are able to see Jesus as a real person, someone approachable who enjoys joking and irony. When you pray, do you do so with an air of formality and distance, as though Jesus is not a person but an abstract concept? Or is it familiar? Are you talking to someone who knows you? Take a moment now to bring one of your needs to Jesus in prayer, but not with an Oliver Twist posture. Instead, do so knowing that God not only loves you – he likes you and is simply fond of you. Let your guard down. Be informal and remember that Jesus had a sense of humor. It may take a few minutes, even a few attempts, to loosen up. And that's OK! As you pray, journal any response you sense God speaking to you.

THE REAL JESUS

DIGGING DEEPER

Re-read verse 30 of this text: "She went home and found her child lying on the bed, and the demon gone." But how? In Mark 5, Jesus gives demons permission to leave a man and enter some pigs. It's a dramatic scene quite different from the one here in Mark 7. Jesus simply says to the girl's mother, "For such a reply, you may go; the demon has left your daughter."

Demonization – the Greek phrase used in the Bible means "having a demon" – is no simple matter. Suspecting demonization, seeing demons manifest, and casting demons out of someone never play out the same way each time. Jesus' deliverance ministry is not cookie-cutter.

Reflect on your familiarity and experience with demonic deliverance. Maybe you grew up in a church that completely mishandled this subject. Perhaps your church background claims demons can't affect Christians. Or maybe this is completely new territory for you. Spend some time journaling through your thoughts on this issue. Ask for God's peace to flood your pondering. And ask him to empower you to do the ministry of setting people free from demonic oppression. If you wish to be equipped in this way, attend the Meeting God 303 and 304 classes.

DAY 5: GETTING PERSONAL

MARK 8:14-8:30 WITH A FOCUS ON 8:27-30

Small talk. You love it, tolerate it, or hate it. The latter, the haters, often eat lunch with a book as their companion, wear headphones while at work, etc. They're comfortable with silence in social situations. As for the rest of us, we've got to fill up that awkward space with what else but small talk!

Do you think Jesus engaged in much small talk? If he did, it's not really documented in the gospels. Instead, he's often found teaching and telling people to pay close attention. But here, in Mark 8:27-30, the context seems more on the small talk end of the communication spectrum. "On the way he asked them, 'Who do people say I am?'" This question is neither confrontational nor personal. It's pretty easy to talk about what other people think. And according to the disciples, people think Jesus is awesome. One of the greats. A prophet!

But then the turning point happens; Jesus makes the question incredibly personal: "Who do you say I am?" Peter answers, "You are the Messiah." The disciples are finally starting to get it: Jesus isn't just announcing the Kingdom – he's the king of it!

In general, how comfortable are you with real talk and personal questions, those that force you to take a stand? Close your eyes and picture taking a walk with Jesus. He turns to you and says, "Who do you say I am?" In that moment, what does your gut tell you to say? By spending a little more time reflecting, is there anything else you want to say about who you think he is? If you were asked this question within earshot of others, would your answer be different than the one you give in private? Journal a response to God. The time for small talk is over. Genuinely open yourself to Jesus; allow him to ask questions that are both personal and real.

THE REAL JESUS

DIGGING DEEPER

Jesus often pleaded with people not to spread the word about him. We get a clue as to why at the very beginning of the gospel. In Mark 1:38, after laying out a plan to preach in nearby villages, Jesus says, "That is why I have come." He came to proclaim the good news of God's Kingdom to Israel. If word about his power over nature, sickness, death, etc., and his disdain for man-made tradition spread too quickly, especially to groups such as the Pharisees and Roman authorities, his preaching mission would be cut short. Those in power would come after him without delay, accusing him of capital offenses. He wanted as much time as possible to share the Good News before inevitably facing the cross.

This means "don't tell anyone" isn't a command we must obey today. We are called to fling the doors of the Kingdom wide open and invite everyone in. This series, which was created in an attempt to clear up confusion about Jesus, is an opportunity to do just that. This week, invite a friend to church. Add creative ways to show people even just a glimpse of the real Jesus. Pray for a sick friend. Bring a meal to a neighbor recovering from surgery. Speak a kind word to an irate customer at work. Tell a family member about the difference God has made in your life. Spread the Word!

NOTES AND REFLECTIONS

NOTES AND REFLECTIONS

THE REAL JESUS

WEEK 4

JESUS THE REVOLUTIONARY

THE REAL JESUS

GETTING STARTED

Go around the room, share your name, and answer these questions: When you hear the word revolutionary what images or periods of history do you think of? What kind of revolutions are most prominent in your mind?

TEACHING OUTLINE

"...You know that those who are regarded as rulers of the Gentiles lord it over them, and their high officials exercise authority over them. Not so with you. Instead, whoever wants to become great among you must be your servant, and whoever wants to be first must be slave of all." - Mark 10:42-44

- Jesus revolutionized how we view **society**.

"On reaching Jerusalem, Jesus entered the temple courts and began driving out those who were buying and selling there. He overturned the tables of the money changers and the benches of those selling doves, and would not allow anyone to carry merchandise through the temple courts. And as he taught them, he said, "Is it not written: 'My house will be called a house of prayer for all nations'? But you have made it 'a den of robbers.'" The chief priests and the teachers of the law heard this and began looking for a way to kill him, for they feared him, because the whole crowd was amazed at his teaching." - Mark 11:15-18

- Jesus revolutionized **who** gets access to God.

"...Wide is the gate and broad is the road that leads to destruction and many enter through it. But small is the gate and narrow is the road that leads to life and only a few find it." - Matthew 7:13-14

- Jesus revolutionizes **what** our lives look like.

Jesus answered them, "Destroy this temple, and I will raise it again in three days." They replied, "It has taken forty-six years to build this temple, and you are going to raise it in three days?" But the temple he had spoken of was his body. After he was raised from the dead, his disciples recalled what he had said. Then they believed the scripture and the words that Jesus had spoken. Now while he was in Jerusalem at the Passover Festival, many people saw the signs he was performing and believed in his name." - John 2:19-23

- Jesus revolutionizes the __WAY__ we get access to God.

DISCUSSION QUESTIONS

Jesus often taught his followers to go against the grain of culture. Has following Jesus' way caused any conflict with a family member, friend, coworker, boss, or professor because of following Jesus? Describe what happened to the group.

Has anyone had anything more extreme like losing a job or losing a relationship because of Jesus?

Jesus can "over turn tables" and causes messes in people's lives to reset them on a new course or priority. Has Jesus made any messes in your life?

What feeling or hesitation do you have knowing that Jesus will make a "mess" of things in your future? Why could this be a really good thing? *We must follow HIS way because is to the best for us*

What advantage do you see in accessing God through a person and not a religion? *Personal between God & a person!*

PRAYER MINISTRY TIME

Consider praying over some of the "messes" that may have taken place in the life of some of the members of the group. It might work best to pair up in groups of two or three to do this. Otherwise, continue as a group in the following:

Then, take some time to consider areas of your life that have become stale, boring, and/or humdrum. Did you think you'd make a bigger contribution in this world, at work, or in your family at this point in your life? We all want to be a part of something bigger than ourselves. Take some time as a group to pray and ask Jesus to provide some ideas about what your group could do together to make your neighborhood, community, or our city a better place. A great way to do this is to participate with the church in our service project. Talk about how you might serve together as a group!

THE REAL JESUS
NOTES AND REFLECTIONS

NOTES AND REFLECTIONS

NOTES AND REFLECTIONS

THE REAL JESUS

DAY 1: YOUR LOSS IS YOUR GAIN

MARK 8:31-9:13 WITH A FOCUS ON 8:34-9:1

What are you willing to do for love? Is there a song that mirrors your commitment to love? Would you walk 500 miles and then 500 more? Is there a mountain high enough to keep you from love? This is a question that the disciples hadn't really considered. At this point in Mark, the disciples believed Jesus was the Messiah. In their mind this meant Jesus is invincible. He will conquer; he will deliver them from oppression. No need to sacrifice or summit mountains for him, right? When Jesus began telling them his reign would look quite different than they expected, the disciples weren't having it. Moreover, Jesus said that to truly follow him, we too must suffer and die.

Sincerely following Jesus often requires sacrifice. At minimum, it requires a willingness to make sacrifices. When Jesus talks about losing life, he's not saying all of his followers must die by martyrdom. Rather, he's saying you should surrender everything about you – the essential parts of you – in order to experience life to the fullest. Does that mean he'll ask you to change jobs, move, adjust your spending habits, start treating your spouse and kids differently, reorient your schedule, modify your language, do something about the world's injustices, etc.? Not necessarily, but we should be willing to do so.

God is not vindictive, looking out for any opportunity to snatch things away. Instead, he beautifully responds to our willingness to sacrifice and let go of important things. This spiritual act frees us to serve him with sincere, focused hearts. He will give to us a life that's more fulfilling than we could ever imagine. Think about how "disciple" and "discipline" share the same root word. It's usually not without pain, but it's worth it. Bobby Caldwell's 1978 song What You Won't Do for Love captures this level of dedication and sacrifice: "In my world only you make me do for love what I would not do."

Sometimes, a simple physical exercise can put us in touch with the spiritual work God is doing within us. Try this: Sit in a quiet place and take a few minutes to reflect on things in life you may have too tight of a grip on. This could be something like your career, a relationship, your child's academic success, your future plans, your car, your gadgets, or your need to please others. Is there something that comes to mind? Something that, if it were taken or you lost control of it, would send you reeling. With your palms facing down, say to God, "I release *my life* to you. Do with it as you will. I take up my cross and follow you. I lose my life for you." Then, with your palms facing up, say, "Jesus, fill me with the beautiful, full life only you can offer." Try doing this twice a week.

DIGGING DEEPER

Consider the things that you believe you've sacrificed because you follow Jesus. Maybe you've sacrificed a certain relationship that you knew wasn't what God wanted for you. Perhaps you sacrificed a career move because you believe God didn't want your family to move town. Maybe you told the truth when it was costly; you suffered consequences for being honest. Looking back over things that cost you something to follow Jesus, what have you gained? What is your relationship with God like because of these sacrifices? God remembers our sacrifices and honors them. We can celebrate what the sacrifices have done in us as well!

DAY 2: A SONG OF FAITH AND DOUBT

MARK 9:14-29 WITH A FOCUS ON 9:20-27

Everyone wants to be deeply understood. The desire to encounter thoughts, feelings, and experiences that are relatable to our own is strong. Poems, movies, and songs often fit the bill. We read a stanza, see the emotion on a character's face, or sing along to the lyrics and remark, "Yes! Someone else understands!" When something mirrors our experiences back to us – the good, the bad, the complex – it is so validating to our humanity. We know we're not alone.

One of the many wonderful things about the Bible is that no matter what's going on in your life, it offers a myriad of spiritual and emotional expressions that can resonate with your experience. For instance, in times of grief, the story of the death of Jesus' friend Lazarus offers some solace. There we find the shortest verse in the Bible, John 11:35, which says, "Jesus wept." Jesus knows something of our grief. Alternatively, when you receive good news after a hard season, a great story in Luke 15 likely resonates. After years of going his own way, with horrible results, a son returns to his father. Full of great joy, the father runs to his son, hugs and kisses him, and throws a large party to celebrate his return. When we have cause to celebrate, God joins in!

The complexity of following Jesus is summed up quite well in Mark 9:24, when the father of a demonized boy loudly proclaims for all to hear, "I do believe; help me overcome my unbelief!" You believe God can move in your life, but will he? There are certain things about Jesus you find easy to believe, but some other things? Not so much. What this amounts to is the song of your heart being a complex melody of faith and doubt: "I do believe; help me overcome my unbelief!"

So far in this series, what has echoed where you are with your faith? Perhaps it was a sermon or something said in one of the videos. Maybe it was a particular devotional. Over the past few weeks, even outside of this series, what has left you feeling understood? A Bible passage? A song? A book? Try writing out the main themes of where your faith currently stands. Maybe even turn it into a poem. It's good to know where you are with faith and doubt, and creative endeavors can often help us get there.

On Christ the solid rock I stand!

DIGGING DEEPER

On this side of eternity, where God's kingdom has broken through but it's not yet here in its fullness, nothing feels permanent. Things are always changing. It can even feel this way regarding manifestations of Jesus' love and power. Yes, God broke through in one particular situation, but that doesn't always mean it's going to be smooth sailing from here on out. Sometimes the relief is temporary. In Mark 9:25, when healing the demonized boy, Jesus commanded the evil spirit to "never enter him again." Sometimes the all-healing "never again" of God, prophesied about in Isaiah 65:17-25 and envisioned in Revelation 21:6 happens right now, in the present age!

The friend whose cancer is in remission: may it never return. The brother in recovery: may he never relapse. The sister healed of PTSD: may she always be able to testify, "I had PTSD." Take some time to pray along these lines for yourself and others, that you'd experience the "never again" expression of the fullness of the Kingdom of God.

Healing + understanding between Carol & Nancy.

THE REAL JESUS

DAY 3: UPSIDE-DOWN

MARK 9:30-50 WITH A FOCUS ON 9:30-37

When children play make-believe, someone is eager to be a prince or princess, but never a peasant. Always royal, never ordinary. Always powerful, never overpowered. While it's mostly innocent when kids play make-believe like this, it also illustrates a dark side of humanity: we naturally tend toward wanting power and position.

In this section of Mark, we learn the disciples thought close association with Jesus the Messiah meant one of them would be made something akin to Vice President or Hand of the King. They were arguing about who among them, via power by proxy, would be "the greatest." But in verses 35-37, Jesus calls them to do something else with this power: be a "servant of all" and consider those with neither status nor prestige – even children – their equals in greatness in the Kingdom of God.

Perhaps, like the disciples, there are places you feel the natural predisposition to be first instead of last. Maybe you find yourself relating only with people whom you think might help you get ahead in life. What might God want you to do instead? There's a lot you can do with any position of influence you may have. You can adopt a "servant of all" approach instead of a self-seeking one. You can let Jesus the revolutionary mess up your life by responding to his call to use your power in a revolutionary upside-down Kingdom sort of way.

Quiet your thoughts and ask God to speak: what is one thing he's calling you to do with some of your influence and power? Perhaps it's to contribute less at work meetings and instead ask women and/or minorities in the room to share their ideas. It could mean serving in an area of need such as volunteering to teach English to immigrants and refugees. You could give someone without a car a ride to church. Upside-down tactics of the kingdom can be as simple as learning the name of the coffee shop barista, striking up a conversation with the custodian at your child's school, or asking a homeless person to share their story with you. Make a plan to do this one thing and pray that God would continue to direct you in your quest to be "servant of all."

DIGGING DEEPER

In verses 42-50 we see how seriously Jesus takes the values of his Kingdom. Sometimes we can view the upside-down Kingdom of Jesus as a "nice" kingdom or a kingdom of pleasantries. But Jesus reveals the direness and the magnitude of living in this revolutionary way. Pluck out your eye? Cut off your hand? Cut off your foot?

There is a temptation to look at the teachings and ways of Jesus as good advice. But according to the real Jesus, it is the only way to live a fully satisfied life. It is the only way to be fully human. It takes serious resistance to our natural bents in order to receive the freedom only Jesus can give. Take a few moments and reflect on when you have taken Jesus' words as non-negotiable instead of just a good option. What about the opposite? What areas of your life do you sense the Lord highlighting? Discuss these revelations with a friend from small group. How can you help each other take Jesus seriously?

THE REAL JESUS

DAY 4: I DON'T WANT TO GROW UP

MARK 10:1-16 WITH A FOCUS ON 10:13-16

Aging often rewards one with qualities like patience and wisdom. Being an adult can also offer lots of advantages, like freedom to choose. Nobody tells a 25-year-old when to go to bed or limits screen time for a retiree or instructs a mom on when to eat dinner. Children are usually not wise enough to make these decisions In this way, they are at a disadvantage regarding freedom to choose.

Spiritually speaking though, children often have an advantage over adults. While they were among those seen as "less valuable" in ancient cultures, Jesus' revolutionary Kingdom usually reorients the value of people, and children are no exception. We see this here in Mark 10: Jesus invites children – people undervalued in his day just as many people groups today are – to swarm him. The Kingdom of God belongs to the lowly. In verse 15 Jesus is basically saying, "If you don't get low, my Kingdom isn't the place for you."

Picture verse 16 in your mind's eye and journal what you see – maybe even sketch a picture if you're artistically inclined. Is Jesus standing or kneeling? How many children are present? Are they jumping around? Are they yelling? What is their age range? Is Jesus picking them up? Is he putting his hands on their heads? What is the blessing; is it spoken or unspoken? Is there a particular child who catches your eye? Why?

How can we become these children in Jesus' arms, receiving his blessing? Do we recognize our need for a savior? Do we recognize the greatness of who he is? Are there things that might get in the way, such as self-sufficiency? Ask God to reveal one hurdle – be it something that hardens your heart, distracts you, scares you, etc. – that keeps you at a "disadvantage" from receiving him. Visualize laying this down on the ground, then turning to Jesus as he scoops you up into his arms.

THE REAL JESUS

DIGGING DEEPER

Let's look at the context of these few verses. Just before the disciples rebuke children for swarming Jesus, Mark tells us the story of him answering the Pharisees' questions about divorce. Jesus was aware that the Jewish people had altered Moses' original permissions for divorce. Over time they had expanded divorce permissions to what is commonly referred to as "no fault" divorce or "divorce for any reason." Jesus then tests their hearts by asking them if they support the "spirit" (intent) of the law or the "letter" (textual limits) of the law. In other words, Jesus wants to know if their hearts are toward God's intentions or using the text of the law to their sinful advantage. They respond by repeating the text. He responds by giving the purpose God gives for marriage.

What does it mean for you to follow the spirit instead of the letter? Is there an area where your freedom has been used unwisely and therefore led to harm? If so, take some time to repent before the Lord and receive his forgiveness.

follow GOD'S LAW

NOT MANS SINFULL REASONING

THE REAL JESUS

DAY 5: FIRST PLACE

MARK 10:17-31

"What must I do to inherit eternal life?" The rich man in this story asked the wrong question. Yes, it's perfectly fine to be curious about eternity – the age to come, the Kingdom of God – but his question smells of religion, of a desire to check off a box and be on his merry way. He had the ear of Jesus the Messiah, the most captivating and powerful person to ever live, and he chose to ask a question about religious scorekeeping.

Beginning in verse 21, as Jesus starts to unpack the man's question on a deeper level, thus telling him what it really takes to be part of the age to come, notice Jesus' first response is a silent, emotional one: he "looked at him and loved him." This is the real Jesus, a person abounding in compassion, even when we are way off track.

Indeed, Christians can find themselves getting off track. So often we subconsciously tally up our "goods" and our avoidance of "bads". This can, and often does, play into what we believe we have earned from God. The rich man believed by obeying the commandments, he had earned entrance into the Kingdom of God. Jesus reveals that entrance into the Kingdom of God requires releasing that which challenges Jesus as holding first place in your life. Only he is worthy to fill that spot. Sure, the rich struggle with their riches. But all struggle with giving God first place. All struggle to release that which is precious.

The real Jesus looks at you and loves you right now, as you continue your journey toward discovering who he really is. Even though you may get off track at times, you are his beloved. Take a moment now to picture Jesus looking at you, with a soft expression of kindness and love in his eyes. How do you feel? Journal a response, perhaps including a few new questions for Jesus.

DIGGING DEEPER

The list of what can seriously compete for first place varies. For you it could be wealth, power, sex, pleasing people, your looks, your children, your desire for children or a spouse, politics, food, fitness, shopping, education, video games, etc. The man was fiercely attached to his wealth. And since he couldn't fit it through the doorway to the Kingdom, he decided to bail. To echo Peter in verse 28, he was not willing to leave everything and follow Jesus.

To be clear, Jesus wasn't telling the man he'd earn his way into the Kingdom by giving all his stuff away. Rather, it was his extreme love for his wealth and its centrality to his identity that needed released. It got in the way of his ability to receive the kingdom. With that in mind, isolate the five one-word commands Jesus issues to the man in verse 21: go, sell, give, come, and follow. Spend a few minutes in silence. Then, using these words, write the command you believe Jesus is speaking specifically to you.

NOTES AND REFLECTIONS

NOTES AND REFLECTIONS

THE REAL JESUS

WEEK 5

JESUS THE SUFFERING SERVANT

THE REAL JESUS

GETTING STARTED

Go around the room, share your name and one thing that you have learned about Jesus or yourself in the last four weeks. How has what you've learned impacted you?

TEACHING OUTLINE

Jesus as Messiah

"For even the Son of Man did not come to be served, but to serve and to give his life as a ransom for many." - Mark 10:45

"Jesus and his disciples went on to the villages around Caesarea Philippi. On the way he asked them, "Who do people say I am?" They replied, "Some say John the Baptist; others say Elijah; and still others, one of the prophets." "But what about you?" he asked. "Who do you say I am?" Peter answered, "You are the Christ (Messiah)." - Mark 8:27-29

"He then began to teach them that the Son of Man must suffer many things and be rejected by the elders, chief priests, and teachers of the law, and that he must be killed and after three days rise again. He spoke plainly about this, and Peter took him aside and began to rebuke him." - Mark 8:31-32

- The Messiah must suffer to __SAVE__ us.

- The Messiah must suffer to demonstrate his __LOVE__.

"This is how we know what love is: Jesus Christ laid down his life for us." - 1 John 3:16

Making Jesus your Messiah

- Have you accepted his __RANSOM__ for you?

- Have you begun a __RELATIONship__ with him?

THE REAL JESUS

DISCUSSION QUESTIONS

Are you surprised to hear that Jesus describes the purpose of his life "to serve and give his life as a ransom for many?" How does that differ from many leaders today?

Why did Jesus say that he must suffer and die? *to pay for my sins*

Have you answered Jesus' question, "who do you say I am?" What would you answer? *Jesus my Saviour*

What does it look like to have a relationship with Jesus be central to your life?

Jesus is everything to me. He is God!
My friend
Saviour
guide
teacher
etc

PRAYER MINISTRY TIME

The HOST should lead this prayer ministry time. This could be a sacred moment in your group and in your life. Start this time by having each person ask the questions posed at the end of the video: Have I begun a relationship with Jesus? Have I accepted his life and sacrifice?

In the quiet of considering those words, pray and invite God's presence into these moments as we have each time: "Holy Spirit, come. We invite you here. We want to know and experience the real Jesus." Provide some moments of quiet reflection and then ask, "Is there anyone here who would like to begin a relationship with Jesus?"

If someone responds and says yes, lead them through simple prayer: "Jesus, you are a suffering servant and you made a way for me. Would you come into my life and take away my sin and brokenness? Thank you for what you've done for me. Help me to live for you!"

If no one responds, don't be discouraged. Simply invite people to experience the love of God in a fresh way. Remind your group that Jesus loves them deeply and he wants a relationship with them. Have the group stand up in a circle and ask them to hold their hands open, in a posture of receiving something. Have each person pray for the person on her/his right that she/he would experience the radical love of God.

NOTES AND REFLECTIONS

NOTES AND REFLECTIONS

NOTES AND REFLECTIONS

THE REAL JESUS

DAY 1: SERVE LIKE A ROCK STAR

MARK 10:32-52 WITH A FOCUS ON 10:35-45

Musicians normally build a tour around anchor dates such as well-attended festivals and concerts in large cities. If you think of Jesus and the disciples as a band on tour, Jerusalem as the last stop is not only symbolic, it's the only logical end for a successful run. It's where the deliverer, the promised Messiah would establish his reign. It was the spiritual destination place for all Jews – the city where God resided and ministered to his people. Psalm 137:5-6 reads like a love letter from God's people to their beloved city: "If I forget you, Jerusalem, may my right hand forget its skill…" Jesus and his entourage have done the festival circuit, and they've done the hard work of touring to build up a following; it's time for the grand finale to happen in Jerusalem. But once there, Jesus is going to perform a new song that no one thought he'd sing. It will redefine what comprises fame and power. He will suffer instead of conquer. The people wanted an arena rock anthem, and he's about to sing a different tune.

In this passage from Mark 10, James and John seem eager to live large like rock stars that sell out arenas, and to roll into Jerusalem like they own the place. They wanted to flank Jesus in what they assumed would be his glorious triumph, to become prominent when he established his reign. But this sort of extravagant lifestyle holds no resemblance to the life Jesus intends for his followers. He tells us how to live in verses 42-45. To be great you must be a servant. Go to the back of the line. Give away your life to others. Sing a new song.

THE REAL JESUS

Just because Jesus doesn't want you to pursue self-seeking fame and riches, it doesn't mean you are destined to a life of drudgery. As Jesus had a call on his life, so do you. Only you can impact the world in the unique way God designed you to. Look at your talents, giftings, relationships, connections, environment, etc., through the lenses of servanthood. Wherever you are and whatever you're doing, you are on special assignment from God to serve others. You are on tour, debuting a new song to the world, the one God gave you to sing. Look at your calendar and plans for this week. What opportunities are there to wholeheartedly serve others? As you enter into these situations, say a silent prayer: "This is the assignment you've given me. May I complete it with a posture of servanthood, just as Jesus would."

DIGGING DEEPER

On the road to Jerusalem, Jesus was walking into something that would be incredibly difficult and take tremendous sacrifice. We too may go through seasons like this. You may be in one right now, or have a loved one who is. A pregnant friend learns her baby will be born with special needs; you bring your elderly parent, recently diagnosed with Alzheimer's, home to live with you; your company is downsizing; your spouse begins cancer treatments; a loved one begins serving a prison sentence.

Bring a few of these situations – your own and those of loved ones – to mind and hold them before the Lord. Spend at least three minutes praying for each person, pausing often to listen for God's voice. If you sense him speaking anything, write it down and consider sharing it with whomever you sense it applies to.

THE REAL JESUS

DAY 2: 604,800 SECONDS

MARK 11:1-33 WITH A FOCUS ON 11:1-11

The first 10 chapters of Mark, which we've just completed, cover several years of Jesus' life, beginning with his baptism and mission launch and ending with his entry to Jerusalem. So much has happened: calling, healing, deliverance, debates, confusion, explanation, teaching and storytelling, displays of power, etc. True to the fast-paced way Mark likes to tell the story of Jesus, at times it's felt like a blur.

Now we are going to slow down. Way down. But just because we're reducing the pace, things certainly aren't getting simpler. It's not like the cool down at the end of a workout. While the first 10 chapters cover several years these last six chapters of Mark detail just one week (604,800 seconds), the final days of Jesus' life, and they are intense. Generally speaking, the more time and space the Bible allots to addressing a topic, the more important it is to God, the more important it is for us to "get it." With six chapters devoted to one week of Jesus' life, there's a lot for us to "get" here.

In keeping with this pace, slow down and pay really close attention to Jesus' arrival in Jerusalem as detailed here in Mark 11:1-11. Slowly and out loud, read the text two or three times. Journal through the following observations:

- Why do you think Jesus' plans often involved reliance on others, such as the need to borrow a colt? *Jesus had no worldly possessions of His own.*

- Only for the royal are cloaks spread out on the ground; why did the people think of Jesus as royal? *they expected a King.*

- Camp out on the word "Hosanna" for a bit; it's a complex proclamation of exuberant praise, coupled with a prayer for God's salvation, right here, right now. During what times in your life would it have been appropriate to cry out "Hosanna!" to God? *Worship, praise, Joy*

THE REAL JESUS

- In verse 11, when Jesus "looked around at everything," he is taking in the Passover festival scene. Bring to mind festivals you've attended. Were your senses overloaded? What did you see, hear, smell, taste, etc.? *Food, Friends, Noise, Joy.*

- Jesus retreats outside the city walls to a nearby village with his friends. Do you think he wanted to stay in a quiet place? Or was there no space available in the packed city? Where would you want to spend the night?

DIGGING DEEPER

Mark's unpacking of these crucial details comes from "looking back" and retelling the story. He and others have had time to process the significance of those details.

Think back to critical periods in your life. Maybe it was the period leading up to you becoming a Christian or your first week of college. If you're married, it could be the week leading up to your wedding or if you're a parent, the weeks of preparation for the new baby. It may be the time leading up to the loss of a parent or grandparent due to a long illness. If you were retelling this period of time in your life, what details help tell your story? What elements can you look back and see God highlighting as poignant? What can you say Jesus was doing in these details? *Preparing, planning, waiting, anticipating*

Journal your responses to these questions and consider sharing them with a friend in your small group.

THE REAL JESUS

DAY 3: STORYTIME 201

MARK 12:1-27 WITH A FOCUS ON 12:1-12

LOST, a popular television series, followed the survivors of a plane crash on a mysterious island in the South Pacific. Over six seasons, the suspense, complete with lots of supernatural and sci-fi elements, kept viewers hooked each week. However, the 2010 series finale received mixed reviews. Mike Hale of The New York Times said the episode, more than anything else, exemplified how the show was "shaky on the big picture." Several of the writers for LOST have since admitted that they "were making it up as they went along."

Literary critics claim the best stories are written when the author begins by already knowing the ending. Writers who abide by this practice are able to avoid rambling and inconsequential side stories. Jesus knew the ending to the parable he told in this passage, but he also knew the ending to his story – the unfolding story of how he is going to heal the whole world – the big story, the one that matters most.

Unlike The Parable of the Sower in Mark 4, this one about the tenants in Mark 12 doesn't have a happy or fruitful ending. It's a tragic story about being betrayed by the ones you hoped would embrace you. After killing multiple servants, the tenants don't even spare the owner's son. The murdered servants symbolize the Old Testament prophets, people who heard from God and spoke on his behalf about living rightly. Many prophets were not well-received in their time. God's people resisted their call to repentance; they hated their rebukes for not living the way God designed. The murdered son represents Jesus. Finally, the tenants symbolized the Jewish nation as a whole across history and more narrowly the religious experts of Jesus' day. And, according to verse 12, they knew it.

What if you could write your own story of embracing the person and message of Jesus? If you were starting with the end in mind, what ending would you write for Jesus and yourself? What aspects of your character do you need to allow Jesus to work on before that ending can come to fruition? Have there been any messages or messengers that you've rejected along the way? What will you do with the vineyard you have been given? Sit and imagine and then offer some prayers about your future.

DIGGING DEEPER

One of the ways Jesus expertly weaves a story to its ending is by connecting it to the listeners' past. The Parable of the Tenants echoes Isaiah 5:1-7. Furthermore, Jesus quotes Psalm 118:22-23 to help explain the ultimate fate of the murdered son. Take some time to study these texts alongside the parable. Note similarities and differences. How do you think these connections impacted the original audience? How do they impact you today?

THE REAL JESUS

DAY 4: UPWARD AND OUTWARD LOVE

MARK 12:28-44 WITH A FOCUS ON 12:28-34

To understand the real Jesus, we mustn't forget that he was a Jew living in first century Palestine. His Jewishness and time in history are critical to his identity. We wear the lenses of our current culture and era when we look at Jesus's life and ministry. This may make the task of understanding his true purpose in certain biblical passages more difficult. Historical and religious context matters, deeply.

In Jesus' day, Judaism was diverse. There were different sects, such as Pharisees, Sadducees, Zealots, and Essenes. Then came followers of John the Baptist with followers of Jesus not far behind. Just as all religions today have many sects, so it was with Judaism in first century Palestine. While differing from one another in some aspects of faith, each maintained the following core tenets: following dietary laws, observing the Sabbath, and worshipping at the Temple. Because of purity laws and other highly detailed instructions, Judaism, regardless of sect, always touched the everyday lives of its faithful.

The conversation Jesus had with a religious teacher about "The Greatest Commandment" is a time when Mark really highlights the ancient Jewish cultural context. Instead of emphasizing one of the above-mentioned common tenets, he recited the Shema, the most important prayer in Judaism, one that is still recited multiple times per day by devout Jews and surely ingrained in those of Jesus' day. He then says the second-most important commandment is to love others. Combined, these two commandments sum up the whole of the law.

Jesus's response – and the man's understanding of it – speak deeply to the title of this series: The Real Jesus: A Person not a Religion. Christ, while definitely Jewish, had no interest in perpetuating the burdensome teachings of the religious experts of his day. Getting in touch with the real Jesus is not about following an inordinate amount of rules. Instead, it's been distilled down to loving God and loving others, the plan that God had for us all along. When we focus on these two things we are "not far from the Kingdom of God."

As you've journeyed through this series, when have you found yourself filled up and empowered by God to follow these greatest commandments? How have you loved God? How have you loved others? Ask God to give you one idea to take this upward and outward love to the next level. Spend a minute in silence, asking him to speak. How does he want you to get even closer to the Kingdom?

DIGGING DEEPER

In The Parable of the Good Samaritan, found in Luke 10, Jesus explains that a loving neighbor is one who enters into the messiness and suffering of others and extends extravagant mercy. It's a great story, but it should also be a lesson we implement in our own lives.

There's a great book by Mile High Vineyard pastor Jay Pathak called The Art of Neighboring: Building Genuine Relationships Right Outside Your Front Door. On a very practical level, starting with learning the names of all your immediate neighbors, it walks you through how to love and extend mercy to those physically nearby. If you sense the Lord putting his finger on the command to love others, read this book and put some of its ideas into practice.

DAY 5: KEEP WATCH, BE LIKE JESUS

MARK 13:1-37 WITH A FOCUS ON 13:32-37

On September 11, 2001, for that entire horrific day, most of us were glued to a television somewhere watching news of the attack, united in silence, shock, and grief. Quickly, in the days that followed, public libraries across the country began receiving the same inquiry, over and over again: "Do you have any books on Nostradamus?" Completely made up (or, at best, grossly mistranslated) predictions of the 9/11 attack, attributed to this 16th century physician and seer, were speedily making the rounds on the Internet and beyond. People seemed hungry to consume anything about predictions of the attacks as a way of better understanding the events or to better plan for future events.

Fascination with predictions of catastrophic events and the End Times is nothing new. Millenia before Nostradamus, an ancient calendar of the Maya civilization supposedly claimed a "world age" would come to an end on December 21, 2012. Human beings are naturally curious and find comfort in knowing what to expect, so interest in predictions of significant and catastrophic events across cultures and eras is not surprising. But just because it's not surprising, does it mean it's good? Is it something that should preoccupy our thoughts and conversations?

In this text, "that time" Jesus is talking about refers not to the end of the world but to the end of the Jewish nation's way of life. Specifically, in 70 CE, in response to a rebellion, the Roman government would destroy the Temple – the very center of Jewish identity. That said, we can apply his advice and warnings here to all the inevitable unknowns we face. Is Jesus telling us to hunker down and study prophetic timetables? No. What will happen and when it will happen is only for God to know. What does he want us to do instead? Keep watch; stay woke. Be the people he calls us to be. Be like Jesus.

No matter your stage of life, no matter how close we are to Jesus' return, every moment is a chance to be faithful to God and always on the lookout for how he is at work in you and in the world around you. If you're stuck in the headspace of worrying about the future, allow Jesus to beckon you back to the present. Ask him to open your eyes to what he's doing in your midst, right now. How can you join him in this mission? Your "assigned task" may be raising young children, getting a college degree, working for a demanding boss, volunteering for a nonprofit, leading a small group, or all of the above! God wants you to wake up to how he's at work in all of these areas.

DIGGING DEEPER

Perhaps in the early years of your faith you did an excellent job keeping watch. You saw God at work and responded accordingly. Your prayers were bountiful and freely offered to others. Your faith was consistently in action and your heart was overflowing with God's love. But then life took over: a demanding career, a new house to decorate, relationships to nurture, kids to raise, tragedies to endure, illnesses to recover from, etc. You are not as spiritually alert as you once were.

Read the lyrics or listen to the song Fall Afresh by Jeremy Riddle. This is the heart's cry of the one stricken by burdens or apathy. Sing it or pray it as your own petition to God, perhaps a few times. You may want to further engage by kneeling, raising your hands, confessing your sin of apathy or distraction out loud to God, etc.

NOTES AND REFLECTIONS

NOTES AND REFLECTIONS

THE REAL JESUS

WEEK 6

JESUS THE KING

THE REAL JESUS

GETTING STARTED

Go around the room, share your name, and what you believe are the most necessary qualities in a great leader.

TEACHING OUTLINE

"After Jesus was born in Bethlehem in Judea, during the time of King Herod, Magi from the east came to Jerusalem and asked, "Where is the one who has been born king of the Jews? We saw his star when it rose and have come to worship him." - Matthew 2:1-2

"Then the King will say to those on his right, 'Come, you who are blessed by my Father; take your inheritance, the kingdom prepared for you since the creation of the world. For I was hungry and you gave me something to eat, I was thirsty and you gave me something to drink, I was a stranger and you invited me in, I needed clothes and you clothed me, I was sick and you looked after me, I was in prison and you came to visit me.'" - Matthew 25:34-36

"Pilate had a notice prepared and fastened to the cross. It read: Jesus of Nazareth, the king of the Jews. Many of the Jews read this sign, for the place where Jesus was crucified was near the city, and the sign was written in Aramaic, Latin and Greek. The chief priests of the Jews protested to Pilate, "Do not write 'The King of the Jews,' but that this man claimed to be king of the Jews." Pilate answered, "What I have written, I have written." - John 19:19-22

"As they approached Jerusalem and came to Bethphage and Bethany at the Mount of Olives, Jesus sent two of his disciples, saying to them, "Go to the village ahead of you, and just as you enter it, you will find a colt tied there, which no one has ever ridden. Untie it and bring it here. If anyone asks you, 'Why are you doing this?' say, 'The Lord needs it and will send it back here shortly.'" - Mark 11:1-3

- _Partnership_ to Jesus the King

"They went and found a colt outside in the street, tied at a doorway. As they untied it, some people standing there asked, "What are you doing, untying that colt?" They answered as Jesus had told them to, and the people let them go." - Mark 11:4-6

- _Co-workers_ with Jesus the King

"For we are God's co-workers; you are God's field, God's building." - 1 Corinthians 3:9

"Many people spread their cloaks on the road, while others spread branches they had cut in the fields. Those who went ahead and those who followed shouted, "Hosanna!" "Blessed is he who comes in the name of the Lord!" "Blessed is the coming kingdom of our father David!" "Hosanna in the highest heaven!" - Mark 11:8-10

"Some of the Pharisees in the crowd said to Jesus, "Teacher, rebuke your disciples!" "I tell you," he replied, "if they keep quiet, the stones will cry out." - Luke 19:39-40

- _Worship_ of Jesus the King

He is my King!

THE REAL JESUS

DISCUSSION QUESTIONS

How do you imagine God working his purposes in the world?
HIS SERVANTS

Why might God choose to partner with us to accomplish his purposes? *HE IS NOW IN HEAVEN. NOW HE WORKS THREW HIS BELIEVERS,*

How can you be a co-worker together with Jesus the King right now? *By LISTENING TO HIM AND OBEYING*

How do you honestly feel when someone gets emotional during worship or when they talk about Jesus? How do you feel when someone is extravagant in their worship (using their body, clapping loudly, or shouting)? What causes people to worship in this way? *uncomfortable Holy Spirit?*

If you consider Jesus your king, what is the most difficult area to make available to Him and his purposes?
Trusting GOD For proper words

JESUS THE KING

THE REAL JESUS

PRAYER MINISTRY TIME

Start ministry time by saying these familiar words: "Holy Spirit, come. We invite you here. We want to know and experience the real Jesus."

Pair in groups of two or three and answer these questions:
Are there any areas of your life that are not available to Jesus? *words*
Is there any place in your life where you need to give your *Trust* allegiance to Jesus? Ask the Lord: What do you want me to do with my stuff? With my spare bedroom that's not being used? With the resources Jesus has given me? With the clothes I haven't worn in years in my closet? Ask Jesus: what do you want to do with my life? Pray over some of these things together.

Finally, as the HOST, take a moment to offer thanks to God for each person in your group, for being part of the group, participating, and sticking with it. If you've seen particular gifts in people in your group, speak that into their lives to encourage them.

NOTES AND REFLECTIONS

NOTES AND REFLECTIONS

THE REAL JESUS

DAY 1: UNINHIBITED

MARK 14:1-31 WITH A FOCUS ON 14:1-11

Royalty and formality go together like tacos and Tuesdays. This is most apparent at a coronation ceremony, especially those of the past. Beyond taking a long formal vow, a crown was placed on the new ruler's head, followed by presentation of even more regalia, anointing with holy oil, acts of homage, etc. The United Kingdom is the only European monarchy to maintain an elaborate coronation rite, much to the delight of tabloids and British royalty enthusiasts. After 14 months of preparation for Queen Elizabeth II's 1953 coronation ceremony, three million people gathered on London streets to watch the two-mile long procession where the queen wore the 18-feet long Robe of State, with eight maids of honor carrying it behind her.

We've seen some glimpses of Jesus' royalty thus far in the Gospel of Mark. He entered Jerusalem as a king would: on a colt, with people spreading cloaks on the ground in front of him. He even hints at his kingship in his parables. We might expect Jesus to want us to act formally toward him. After all, he is a king! Yet, time and time again Jesus surprises us, causing us to ask, "What kind of king is this?" Whenever people are moved to worship Jesus in Mark, it's done with reverence but seemingly a lack of formality. He loved it when little children ran up to him uninhibited. When overwhelming love for Jesus causes you to spontaneously pour out lavish worship upon him, God smiles at you. Impromptu expressions of worship that lack all inhibition are "beautiful things" unto the Lord. The woman who anoints Jesus at Simon's house in Bethany is a model for us all.

What are some ways you can spontaneously worship and say thank you to God? When the sun finally breaks through after days of dreariness, shout gratitude to God. When you're listening to worship music while cleaning the house, dance for him. When you read something in scripture that penetrates your heart with the truth of just how amazing Jesus really is, pour out your praise. Don't reserve your worship for church services only. Try not to miss any opportunity to do "beautiful things" for God.

DIGGING DEEPER

Mark doesn't paint the other characters in this scene in a very positive light. The religious experts are scheming to arrest and kill Jesus. Others hanging out at Simon's house – the disciples among them – made uncomfortable by the woman's lavish and spontaneous act of worship, show great disdain for her. Opportunistic Judas allies with the chief priests to betray Jesus. Peter would soon follow, in a way, when he disowned Jesus at the cross. We're this far into the gospel story and there still aren't many people who understand and embrace the real Jesus.

Each character is turned inward, focused on their circumstances and motivated to protect their reputations. We can turn inward in small, but dangerous ways, too. Maybe you find yourself cutting corners at work so you can instead take care of personal business or browse social media. Perhaps you miss out on chances to be more present with your kids or your spouse because you're distracted by your phone. As he reveals these things to you, the Holy Spirit is not out to condemn or shame you – he is making space for the transformational act of repentance to take place. Just as Jesus reinstates Peter in John 21, so he wants to do for you.

THE REAL JESUS

DAY 2: YOU'RE MY ONLY HOPE

MARK 14:32-72 WITH A FOCUS ON 14:53-65

There are a few times in our lives where we can't rely on anyone else in order to succeed. When you take your drivers test, there isn't anyone helping you parallel park or check your rear view mirror. Law students can't have a stand-in for the Bar exam. You're on your own.

Charged with crimes punishable by death, Jesus now stood in front of the Sanhedrin, a Jewish court composed of religious leaders. He knew he'd reached the point in his ministry where he was truly on his own. Both human and divine; teacher; healer; revolutionary; paradoxical king donning the mantle of suffering servant: these were what he had as his defense and witness before the court. He was representing humanity, and their eternal fate would rest in his hands. It's hard to imagine the pressure and weight on Jesus' shoulders. The cross and all its brutality were imminent. What got him through it? Hebrews 12:2 gives us insight: "For the joy set before him he endured the cross, scorning its shame, and sat down at the right hand of throne of God."

Perhaps you or someone you're close to is being tested and feeling like "you're on your own" and joy on the other side is hard to imagine. Especially when it's something like crippling debt, loss of someone close to you, marital strife, a wayward child, or chronic disease. We have a representative who has walked farther than us. Having passed the test of suffering and death, life is on the other side for all who attach themselves to him. Ask God to help you envision joy beyond the present circumstances for you or someone you know. What Jesus offers us are not pie in the sky predictions, but assurance that he is with us through our test and on the other side with joy.

THE REAL JESUS

DIGGING DEEPER

Peter, one of Jesus' best friends, is hanging around the fringes of this story. In verse 54, he "followed at a distance" on the way to the Sanhedrin. In this chapter of Peter's discipleship journey and friendship with Jesus, it's safe to say he was of the fair weather variety.

Ask God to reveal any "fair weather friend of Jesus" tendencies residing in you. Maybe this looks like rolling into church late each week. Or maybe you don't regularly attend a small group. Your Bible is gathering dust or you find that turning to God in prayer or pointing co-workers, friends, etc., toward Jesus when the situation warrants it are acts that don't come naturally. Moving away from these tendencies toward intentional engagement makes way for encountering the real Jesus.

This is not about whether God loves you – his love for you is steadfast and strong no matter what. Rather, Jesus longs for you to be more than acquaintances, more than a fair weather friend. What is one way you can deepen your friendship and loyalty to Jesus? Put it into action this week and pray for grace to grow in loyal friendship with the Lord.

THE REAL JESUS

DAY 3: PAIN AND SHAME TRANSFORMED

MARK 15:1-32 WITH A FOCUS ON 15:21-32

Most of us have not seen the brutality of war up close and personal. Those of us who have are changed by its horrors. What makes war so awful is its vivid display of humanity's inhumanity. Civilians killed. Prisoners tortured. Entire cities turned to rubble. God did not design us to harm one another; experiencing and witnessing the extreme harm of war is a brutal assault on our purpose. War puts a spotlight on our unfortunate proclivity to dishonor those made in the image of God. Casualties of war are felt even in its survivors, many of whom develop PTSD or at least require serious counseling to reconcile what they've experienced. For good reason, many historians, world leaders etc., insist war must and should be the very last resort.

Jesus is the perfect expression of humanity; he is the chief image-bearer of God. Yet, like the dishonor war inflicts on people, he was not honored by his fellow humans. Sentenced to die by crucifixion for being "King of the Jews," something that threatened both the religious establishment and the Roman occupiers, Jesus' death was purposefully public and humiliating. Like a prisoner of war in the hands of brutal and sadistic enemy forces, he was beaten, stripped naked (unlike the quaint-by-comparison medieval paintings depicting Jesus in a loincloth), too weak to carry the crossbeam, mocked, insulted, and jeered. One detail we may not think of in this story is that Father God was there. Just as he looked at Jesus during his baptism and proclaimed, "You are my Son, whom I love; with you I am well pleased," that's what he says to him on the cross. As people heaped unthinkable pain and humiliation on Jesus, God was there affirming his Son in his purpose and calling.

God didn't shy away from his Son's humiliation on the cross. Instead, the humiliation, pain, and dishonor unleashed on Jesus was the avenue by which we receive reconciliation, redemption, and restored honor. What was meant to harm and shame, God turned to our benefit. Are there moments of shame in your own life that God wants to redeem? What painful events could God enter into, to show you he loves you and to cause something good to come out of it? Sit in silence for a few moments, visualizing handing your hurt over to God.

DIGGING DEEPER

Despite knowing it would cost him his life, Jesus did not reject the title "king of the Jews." Written on the sign hanging above him on the cross, people seized upon it, using it to mock him. And yet, it is a true title. Jesus is king of everything, if we allow him to be.

Think about the role Jesus plays in your life and fill in the blank: king of _____. Is he king of your finances? Or would that require generosity that's outside your comfort zone? Is he king of your sexuality? Or would it be social suicide to pursue sexual purity in this stage of life? Is he king of your five-year plan? Or would that mean walking away from a lucrative career track? Is he king of your retirement plans? Or would that mean the life of leisure you've been waiting for now becomes one of service? Pray God would help you keep your eyes on the long-term gains that more than offset the loss of making Jesus king of everything: increased closeness to him, greater fruitfulness in ministering to others, less overall drama in your life, peace that surpasses understanding, etc.

THE REAL JESUS

DAY 4: AN UNLIKELY SOURCE

MARK 15:33-47 WITH A FOCUS ON 15:33-41

"Has anything you've done made your life better?" In the film American History X, this is the question posed to character Derek Vinyard at the tipping point of his departure from Neo-nazism. While in prison serving a term for manslaughter, he grows increasingly conflicted about his hateful convictions. Torn about his beliefs and tormented by his past, he seems to be on the precipice of change. Derek's former high school principal visits him in prison and persuades him to reject hatred and warns him that his younger brother Danny, who idolizes Derek, is following in his dangerous footsteps. The principal asks, "Has anything you've done made your life better?" Derek then breaks down in tears, expressing a desire to change. Once released, he is committed to save his brother with a message of peace, truth, and love.

Proclamations of truth from an unlikely source, like a former Nazi gang leader telling you to seek racial reconciliation, cause us to do a double take. It's never what we expect. In verse 39 of this passage, the centurion, a Roman army officer, declares Jesus is the Son of God. In Mark, he was the first person to do this. A man of prestige and power saw Jesus tried, convicted, beaten, humiliated, mocked, and die a brutal death; yet his conclusion was, "Surely this man was the Son of God!" In Jesus' death he saw truth. Double take time! Of all people, how could this Roman soldier be the first bearer of this good news?

THE REAL JESUS

This is Mark's way of telling us that God's invitation is open to all; anyone can proclaim Jesus is the Son of God, the king. You may think you don't fit the mold of someone who would follow Jesus; the Roman centurion certainly didn't, but look at how God moved in his life! Jesus delights in calling unlikely people to himself. Recontextualize the question Derek's principal asks in American History X. No matter what your background, no matter what gives you pause, is anything in your life better than receiving the Kingdom of God through faith in Jesus? Is anything better than the chance to do life with the real Jesus, the person who is healing the world? Pray your eyes would be opened as the centurion's were; tell Jesus what truths you see in his death. Say yes to his invitation to the Kingdom.

DIGGING DEEPER

Take some more time to reengage the level of sacrifice endured by Jesus. Slowly read this passage again, out loud. Do so at least two times. Stop to ponder each of these events: Jesus' crying prayer, the crowd's misunderstanding, Jesus' last breath, the tearing of the temple curtain, the centurion's confession, and the women watching from a distance.

Devote the biggest chunk of time to Jesus' words in verse 34. He was subject to absolute brutality, something that was part of God's plan, and yet he still remained in communication with his father instead of writing him off. When given opportunities to reject God in seasons of suffering, think about what it would look like to stay in communion with him instead. How can you cultivate such a posture in your life?

THE REAL JESUS

DAY 5: WET PAINT

MARK 16:1-20 WITH A FOCUS ON 16:1-8

My family once commissioned a local artist to create an oil painting for my grandfather as a Christmas gift. It was a wooded landscape featuring white-tailed deer, a nod to my grandfather's passion for the outdoors and hunting. I came home one day to find the painting complete, hanging in my parents' bedroom. Eager for a closer look, I walked right up to it and admired the color and texture. Upon touching it I immediately realized the paint was still wet! It wasn't fully done yet!

At the end of the Gospel of Mark, Jesus is risen! The story of his life is finished. Or is it? In the earliest known manuscripts of Mark, the ending is abrupt, cut short. It's as though a page is missing. What did Jesus do after he rose from the dead? How did his wider circle of friends respond to his resurrection? We need more information!

Interestingly, and perhaps providentially, this presents us with an opportunity. Think of the Gospel of Mark, particularly its ending, as a wet canvas handed to us by God. It depicts several characteristics of the real Jesus – his humanity; his teaching gift; his healing power; his revolutionary agenda; his suffering and servitude; his kingship – but it is an incomplete story of the Kingdom of God. The painting isn't quite done yet. The story is still in progress. And we all have a part to play.

THE REAL JESUS

Consider the brushstrokes you can add to Jesus' story, both right now and over time: your response to his resurrection; whether you will follow him with everything that's in you; whether you will return to him after seasons of forsaking him – something Peter was specifically invited to do in verse 7; how this series has impacted your beliefs about God; where you are right now on your spiritual journey; what you will tell others about the experience; your role in helping others receive the Kingdom of God, etc. Write these brushstrokes down in the form of words, and pray that whatever God has deposited in you over the course of this series would last and multiply.

DIGGING DEEPER

Take some time to look through all of your notes in this workbook: those you recorded during small group meetings and the ones you wrote while using these devotionals. Underline whatever maintains a grip on you. Do you notice any themes?

What do you think the Lord is speaking to you through this? Quiet your thoughts and sit before him in silence for a minute or two. You've done your own underlining; what is he underlining?

What action do you sense him asking you to take as a result of this revelation? Find out whether friends in small group or at church are feeling led in the same direction. Make a plan to walk it out, ideally with at least one other person.

THE REAL JESUS
NOTES AND REFLECTIONS

NOTES AND REFLECTIONS

THE REAL JESUS
NOTES AND REFLECTIONS